"I love this book. Written by someone who has lived what she challenges her readers to do, the 'how tos' are both practical and creative. Every pastor should have a copy, then all church missions committee members, and finally all believers serious about their faith. Just the right length and just the right tone."

—David R. Mains, director of Mainstay Ministries,
Carol Stream, Illinois

"This is a dangerous book! Dangerous to the powers of darkness that would wish to keep old, outdated images of missionaries intact. Donna Thomas blows apart old stereotypes with her very practical and winsome book that will help you raise future missionaries. This is a very encouraging book for any family with an action plan for outwardness."

—Steve Sjogren, founding pastor,
Vineyard Community Church, Cincinnati, Ohio

"*Becoming a World Changing Family* covers all the bases for a family to make a difference in this world: biblical, prayer, creative activities, and involvement. *Becoming a World Changing Family* can help families put action to the heart for the world that God has given them! *Fun, creative, practical*, and *impactful* are just a few words to describe *Becoming a World Changing Family*. May this resource be used by families for God's glory!"

—Jill Harris, children's mobilization specialist,
Caleb Project, Littleton, Colorado

"Donna Thomas has notched up the fun for every family in this insightful book, and at the same time she challenges families to focus on mission. I highly endorse this book and plan to make it available to families in my local church!"

—Stan Toler, author and pastor, Oklahoma City, Oklahoma

"Full of doable ideas, this book challenges Christian families to know the world they want to change. Donna Thomas maps out simple—and fun—strategies to raise mission-minded kids who will celebrate cultural differences as they build spiritual bonds. No passports required!"

—Holly G. Miller, author, editor, professional in residence, Anderson University

"This book will reshape your view of what it means to fulfill the Great Commission. Donna Thomas offers parents many creative and practical ways of mentoring their children so that they impact their world for Christ. Put this book on the 'must-read' list for every parenting class and missions emphasis in the local church. Higher education institutions will want to add this book to their required reading lists for courses dealing with family life, intercultural studies, and teacher education. I would strongly recommend that every pastor provide this motivating book to every young family within the congregation. It will revolutionize the way we prepare Christian leaders!"

—Dr. John D. Fozard, president, Mid-America Christian University,
Oklahoma City, Oklahoma

"Donna's book will make a wonderful contribution to assist parents in thinking of their children in regard to the world and in finding creative ways of involving them in the lives of missionaries and internationals. Her suggestions are eminently practical, and her personal stories are highly inspirational. This book will be both a wonderful gift and a practical guide for parents and extended family members."

—David Mays, Great Lakes regional director, ACMC
(Advancing Churches in Missions Commitment)

"The author provides for parents a wealth of practical ways to help children know and appreciate people of all cultures around the world and see them through the eyes of Christ. These ideas work! They come right out of the author's own family where she and her husband partnered to provide their sons with a heart for the world."

—Dr. David Cox, pastor emeritus, Church at the Crossing, Indianapolis, Indiana

"It's a big world out there—and, like it or not, it's a world growing smaller, closer, and interdependent. *Becoming a World Changing Family* will help everyone in your house experience the adventure, the excitement, and the challenge of successfully engaging the world beyond our front door for heaven's sake. The book includes a suitcase full of practical ideas to bring the world home and bring Jesus to the world. It is inspiring, fun, biblically grounded, and easy to use, all at once. It is a one-of-a-kind guidebook for all ages. It's a ticket to discovery and a new way of life.

"Opportunity waits just inside the front cover and smiles all the way through to the last page. Don't let this book's promise pass you by: You and your family can literally change the world."

—Jim Lyon, senior pastor, North Anderson Church of God, Anderson, Indiana

BECOMING
A WORLD CHANGING
FAMILY

Fun & Innovative Ways to Spread The Good News

DONNA S. THOMAS

BECOMING
A WORLD CHANGING
FAMILY

Fun & Innovative Ways to Spread The Good News

DONNA S. THOMAS

P.O. Box 55787 Seattle, WA 98155

YWAM Publishing is the publishing ministry of Youth With A Mission. Youth With A Mission (YWAM) is an international missionary organization of Christians from many denominations dedicated to presenting Jesus Christ to this generation. To this end, YWAM has focused its efforts in three main areas: (1) training and equipping believers for their part in fulfilling the Great Commission (Matthew 28:19), (2) personal evangelism, and (3) mercy ministry (medical and relief work).

For a free catalog of books and materials, contact:

YWAM Publishing
P.O. Box 55787, Seattle, WA 98155
(425) 771-1153 or (800) 922-2143
www.ywampublishing.com

Becoming a World Changing Family:
    Fun and Innovative Ways to Spread the Good News

14 13 12 11 10 09 08   10 9 8 7 6 5 4 3 2 1

Published by YWAM Publishing
P.O. Box 55787
Seattle, WA 98155

ISBN-10: 1-57658-452-6
ISBN-13: 978-1-57658-452-1

Previously published by Baker Books

Printed in the United States of America.

To my three sons,
Chuck, Paul, and John,
and my three daughters-in-law,
Sue, Dawn, and Nancy.
A greater joy and deeper pride
no mother could ever know.
You are loved.

CONTENTS

Acknowledgments 11
Foreword by Rev. Claude Robold 13

1. Life in the Fast Lane 15
2. Where Is the World? 23
3. What Is a Great Commission Family? 29
4. What Are Great Commission Kids? 35
5. Let's Have a Party! 49
6. Are Missionaries Real People? 55
7. Fun and Games 61
8. You've Got Mail 67
9. Developing Jesus' Vision 73
10. A World Trip—Locally 87
11. On Your Doorstep 97
12. Investing—Not the Stock Market 107
13. Give It a Try—Short-Term Missions 117
14. A Family Adventure 135
15. The Role of the Extended Family 141
16. The Role of the Church 149
17. God's Messengers 155

Notes 159

ACKNOWLEDGMENTS

I f you could read between every line of this book, you would find the fingerprints of Karen Roberts. As my friend and editor, she spent days, weeks, and months helping me write what I wanted to say, refining my efforts, and encouraging me in the process. Without her this book might never have been written and certainly not published. She is an editor par excellence, and I thank her.

Then there are those who helped me with a particular chapter—I thank Martha Black, Linda Kress, and Kimberly Elliott of White Chapel Church of God in South Daytona, Florida; Barbara Brandt, Laura McCollum, and Ellen Hughes of Church of the Crossing in Indianapolis, Indiana; Stephanee Standefer of Willow Creek Church in Barrington, Illinois; Marilyn Stanley and Zoe Dean Middleton of Western Hills Methodist Church in El Paso, Texas; Sue Thomas of First Baptist Church in Geneva, Illinois; Diana Francis of Evangelical Community Church (EPC) in Cincinnati, Ohio; Wilma Walls and Michele Walters of New Life Community Church in Noblesville, Indiana; and Sarah Wright, Christina Hemp, and Janet C. Smith of Hazel Dell Christian Church in Carmel, Indiana.

For valuable information on their families' involvement in missions, I thank Jim Lyon, Gary Kendall, Cindy Judge, Emmy Stanley, Don Johnson, Kevin Engel, Dave Snyder, Nate Irwin, Paul and Bethel Baumann, Franklin Mayfield, Steve Igarta, Phyllis Cain, Steve Weldon, Stan Lewis, Angie Yoder, David Bulger, Ken Johnson, Dick High, Tony Danhelka, Bruce Roberts, and Mike Harrison.

I offer thanks also to my encouragers Holly Miller, Mary Mandel, Paula Quinn, Betty Harman, and Claude Robold.

Thanks goes as well to my "other family" in the rest of the world who have helped me see, respond to, and enjoy the journey of sharing the Lord's blessings with others—Enrique Cepeda, Pastor Lam, Samuel Stephens, Misael and Amina Lopez, Andrew Bondarenko, Lener Cauper, Jean Joseph Surin, Ali Velasquez, and Guillermo Villanueva.

To my wonderful grandchildren—Heather, Erin, Bryson, Allie, Michael, Johnny, Morgan, Marty, and Nicole—for their response to the Lord and his world, I owe much thanks.

To my loving and supportive family—Paul and Dawn, John and Nancy, Chuck and Sue Thomas, and my husband, Chuck, who is with the Lord—I owe a lifetime of gratitude.

Most of all I thank my heavenly Father, who is my guide and director, my strength and my joy.

FOREWORD

Y ou are about to read a book that could change the course of generations and impact this world for eternity. It is my firm conviction that followers of Jesus Christ have been placed in this world to win and develop others to become world changers. There is no better place to begin than right in our own homes and families.

Author Donna Thomas is a world changer herself. She and her late husband offered me the opportunity to see the world with a greater perspective. I was their pastor, and they invited me to become involved in our world in a larger scope than I had ever thought possible.

Donna continues with the same heart to challenge others to see their place in this world as representatives of Jesus Christ. She has challenged us to begin with the generation immediately following us. Our children and grandchildren face a shrinking global world. They will have opportunities to mold this world that you and I have never experienced.

We have the marvelous experience of shaping young minds and hearts so they will be ready to seize the opportunities to be world changers. *Becoming a World Changing Family* will give you a bountiful supply of ideas about how you can effectively develop a worldview in the lives of your children and grandchildren.

I commend Donna on sharing her heart for our children, our grandchildren, and our world. Her writing comes from years of being a world changer. You will be blessed as you begin to change the view of your children and grandchildren about the world in which they live. You will be able to give them purpose and hope for all they will face in the years to come.

Rev. Claude Robold,
Middletown, Ohio

LIFE IN THE
FAST LANE

Hurry up, kids. We gotta go. Allie! Allie, we'll be late to your music lesson if you don't hurry. Marty, you come, too, so I can drop you off at church. Morgan, Kati's mother is picking you up to take you to gymnastics. Come on! Hurry up! We've got lots to do." Sound familiar? Just change the names and it might be your house.

Parents are consumed with the myriad of activities intended to develop their children. This new century adds stress upon stress; parents must continually evaluate and reevaluate the things that call for their children's attention. Christian parents have an even greater agenda, adding spiritual development to the mix of educational, social, and physical development. Life is hectic. Sometimes we don't know where we are going or have time to think about why, but we are getting there fast.

So how does a family in the fast lane fit God's commands into daily life? It is easy to pick and choose what we want from the Scriptures and somehow neglect the rest. Sometimes we think we know what is best without even seeking God's wisdom. Not that we purposely overlook it, but we're busy, and we often think we know what works best for *our* family. In a nutshell, here's what this book is all about—creative ideas to help you keep the essentials of Scripture foremost in your family's life.

Here's a quick look at the essentials, the basic instructions. The details and creative ideas are in the chapters that follow.

Old Testament Basics

Early in the Old Testament (Exodus 20), God gives us the Ten Commandments. At God's prompting, Moses reviews them in a speech to the people in Deuteronomy 5. Chapter 6 adds this admonition: "Love the LORD your God with all your heart and with all your soul and with all your strength. These commandments that I give you today are to be upon your hearts. Impress them on your children. Talk about them when you sit at home and when you walk along the road, when you lie down and when you get up" (Deut. 6:5–7).

These instructions are straightforward. God's people are to know what he says, to talk about his commands with their children, and to model his instructions in the way they live. The last part of these instructions is especially important to families. If parents don't show their children the importance of God's words, children just might consider those words simply as an option—if they have time, if there is nothing else to do, or if it is convenient for them.

Sometimes our human desires lead us to ignore what the Scriptures tell us to do. Remember the story in the Old

Testament where King Saul got in such a hurry he felt he knew what he should do rather than follow the Lord's directions? In 1 Samuel 15:22, Saul was confronted by a prophet about his disobedience to God: "Does the LORD delight in burnt offerings and sacrifices as much as in obeying the voice of the LORD?" Samuel said to Saul. "To obey is better than sacrifice." Saul's decision to ignore what he knew was right cost him his kingship. He learned the hard way that God's commands weren't optional. Likewise, if we are to do our best for ourselves and our families, we'd better pay attention to these Old Testament basics.

New Testament Basics

In the New Testament, Jesus makes the Old Testament instructions much easier to understand and apply to everyday life. He says, "Love the Lord your God with all your heart and with all your soul and with all your mind. This is the first and greatest commandment. And the second is like it: 'Love your neighbor as yourself'" (Matt. 22:37–39). If we follow those two instructions, he says, we will have done all that God told us in the Old Testament.

That's it? Not exactly. Before he returns to heaven, Jesus makes one additional specific, important statement—what we now call the Great Commission. Jesus tells his disciples, his most loyal followers, "All authority in heaven and on earth has been given to me. Therefore, go and make disciples of all nations, baptizing them in the name of the Father and of the Son and of the Holy Spirit, and teaching them to obey everything I have commanded you. And surely I will be with you always, to the very end of the age" (Matt. 28:18–20). The words "go and make disciples" along with "I have commanded" make up

17

a commandment, a New Testament commandment, called the Great Commission.

Making It Work

That's it, the basic instructions. Now all we have to do is follow them. But how, living as we do in the fast lane?

If we accept what we read in Deuteronomy 6:5–7 as the way to obey God's commands—to follow them and teach them to our children—then our response to the Great Commission part of the basic instructions is twofold. First, it is our responsibility to know the Scriptures. Second, it is our job to teach them to our children. It is not the responsibility of the church, although its help is greatly appreciated. It is not the responsibility of Christian schools or relatives, even though they support and enhance our work. It is the responsibility of parents and a measureless privilege the Lord has given us. *How* we do it is up to us. That is the essence of this book.

Missions, Mission Statements, and the Great Commission

Most corporations today have a mission statement and operating principles that define the purpose and objectives of the corporation. Mission statements and the basic operating principles that rise out of them serve as a guide for decision making and implementation. Corporations owned and run by Christians typically include God's "basic instructions" as part of their identity. Here is an example:

Cornerstone Properties, Inc.

Cornerstone Properties, Inc. is a real estate operating company whose objective is to develop and acquire quality real estate

18

assets, and to provide superior asset and property management services to maximize investment returns.

Operating Principles:
Commitment to Excellence—We shall strive individually and collectively for excellence in all endeavors.

Business Ethics—We shall conduct business in such a manner that our actions shall be judged responsible by third parties and always reflect positively upon the favorable image of the company.

Commitment to Honesty and Integrity—We shall conduct all business in an honest, straightforward manner.

Commitment to the Golden Rule—We shall treat employees, residents, and business associates with respect, and will respond to any questions or concerns with prompt attention.

Commitment to Fair Housing—We shall not discriminate against any person because of race, color, religion, sex, handicap, familial status, or national origin.

Corporate Citizenship—We shall strive to be a responsible corporate citizen in those endeavors that affect the communities in which we operate and serve.[1]

Churches, too, are busy these days crafting and implementing mission statements. The mission of one church in Ohio, for example, is *Developing world Christians who develop world Christians.* That mission statement focuses the church collectively and its people individually on activities directly related to the Great Commission. The church and its people teach, train, send, and give continued support to various missions efforts.

The word *missions*, as it is used in the church and Christian organizations, is not unrelated to the modern emphasis on mission statements. The word has been used to identify and classify the "work" that specifically fulfills the purpose of such organizations or implements their mission statements as they extend their reach into the world doing what Jesus described in Matthew 28—the Great Commission. Webster defines *mission* as "the act or an instance of sending" or "a ministry commissioned to propagate its faith or carry on humanitarian work."[2] It is work in a field of missionary enterprise. In general, *missions* refers to the organized systems for telling other people about Jesus Christ. Missions are called home missions when the work is done in our country and foreign (or international) missions when the work reaches out to other countries. The people involved are called missionaries. A church's missions budget is created to extend financial help systematically to the missions and missionaries it supports.

Individuals develop mission statements as well. Some post them on personal Web pages. One man's mission statement is *Making Christ first in every aspect of my life with his principles of living and relating to others.*

Matthew 28:18–20 is often described as the mission or mission statement of Christians. Jesus told us to go and to make disciples. We also are told to baptize them and teach them. As those we reach accept their responsibility for the Great Commission, God's work increases in such a way that multitudes find Jesus Christ as their Savior and Lord. When we make the Great Commission our mission, we obey God, please him, and develop a legacy for our children and many others whom we may never know.

Fast-Lane Families and the Great Commission

Let's look back at our life in the fast lane, which is sometimes the superfast lane. Clearly it is our responsibility and privilege to know, follow, and help our children know and follow God's basic instructions. These instructions include the Great Commission. So where does a family begin? Creating a family mission statement can be your first step. It will focus your family's attention on living as God wants you to live and on doing all that God requires.

If you haven't done so already, sit down together and write your family mission statement. If you have one already, take time to revisit it. What is your family's purpose? What are its values and desires? How are these values and desires being implemented (or not) in the activities in which your family is involved?

Examining, discussing, and praying about your family's current slate of activities will help you define and refine your family's purpose, values, and desires. Writing them down and reviewing them from time to time will help you make choices with your time, activities, and academic and social lives. Most importantly, taking the step of writing your family mission statement will enable you to give priority to the top priority—what God says about how to live and how to fulfill the Great Commission.

WHAT YOU CAN DO TODAY AS A FAMILY

1. List the activities demanding your and your children's participation. Rate them on a scale of 1–5 (5 being the greatest) as to their long-range, lasting value.
2. List the activities you and your family would like to participate in but have not yet found the way or means to do so. Rate them also on a scale of 1–5.
3. Memorize Deuteronomy 6:6–7. "These commandments that I give you today are to be upon your hearts. Impress them on your children. Talk about them when you sit at home and when you walk along the road, when you lie down and when you get up."
4. Memorize the Great Commission passage, Matthew 28:18–20. "Then Jesus came to them and said, 'All

authority in heaven and on earth has been given to me. Therefore go and make disciples of all nations, baptizing them in the name of the Father and of the Son and of the Holy Spirit, and teaching them to obey everything I have commanded you. And surely I am with you always, to the very end of the age.'"

5. Take time to imagine what kind of people you want your children to become as adult Christians. What single step could you take today to move toward that picture? Do it.

6. As a family, discuss and agree on your family's mission statement. Frame it and place it in a prominent place in your home.

7. Help your children create and write their personal mission statements in the front of their Bible.

WHERE
IS THE WORLD?

Mexico, China, England, Russia, and Germany. You know where they are. What about Spain, Italy, Egypt, Israel, and Afghanistan? Sure you can point to them on a globe. But how about Sri Lanka, Indonesia, Taiwan, Morocco, and Latvia? Few people can instantly locate them. Try Suriname, Chad, Senegal, Belize, and Oman. What about the twelve independent nations that emerged from the breakup of the USSR? Are you getting the idea? The world is a big place—hard to know and constantly changing. To what world did Jesus refer when he said, "Go"?

Our world is not the same as that of our parents. If you were born in 1952, your world held only two and a half billion people. The world's population topped six billion in October 1999, and it is said to be doubling every forty years. Two countries, China and India, each have over a billion people.

Some megacities house millions of people. Sao Paulo, Mexico City, Beijing, Tokyo, Cairo, Hong Kong, London, New York City, Los Angeles, New Delhi, Mumbai, Shanghai, Bangkok, Singapore, and Manila each contain up to twenty-five million people.

Here's another way to look at the world. Look at the hemispheres. The western hemisphere, the Americas, has only 12 percent of the world's population. The U.S. and Canada alone make up 5 percent of that figure. Contrast that information with the rest of the world. Oceania—Australia, New Zealand, and the South Pacific islands—has only one half of one percent of the world's population. Europe has 8 percent. Africa has 15 percent, and Asia has the most with 64 percent.

In the last twenty-five years, communication technology and transportation have given us yet more ways to see the world. They have made a monumental impact on our knowledge and understanding. Consider the options now available in travel, global television, telephones, and mobile phones in far-reaching countries. Now add the Internet. What do you want to know about the world and its people? You can find answers in minutes. You can experience the world firsthand without ever leaving home. Where do you want to go? You can get there by plane in a few hours if you have the money.

Have you heard of the 10/40 Window? It is defined as the area from 10 to 40 degrees north of the equator and from West Africa to East Asia. This area is home to two-thirds of the world's people, the world's three great non-Christian religions, and the majority of the poorest and unreached peoples of the world. The 10/40 Window in recent years has become the focal point for missions efforts. Here's some information compiled as a result of the 10/40 Window missions efforts that might shock you:

- Of each dollar designated for "missions" by American churches, only seventy cents goes overseas. That means thirty cents stays here at home.
- Only two cents of each dollar sent overseas is used to reach the 1.6 billion people throughout the world who have never heard of Jesus Christ. The rest is used on those already reached by the gospel.
- Just one-tenth of a penny of those missions dollars goes to India, where more than one billion people live, the vast majority (85 percent) of whom have not yet heard the gospel.
- Of the 6.5 billion Bibles and New Testaments printed since the invention of the printing press in 1450 A.D., 85 percent have been printed in English. Yet only 21.5 percent of the people in the world speak English.[1]

A Global Society

Countries, states, cities, and even small towns are becoming part of a vast and growing global society. People are moving from place to place, even country to country, with rapid speed. England and European countries are experiencing an influx of multitudes of people coming from Africa, China, the Middle East, and Asia. In our own country, tremendous waves of people come from every part of the world. Their presence is redefining our lives and our communities.

Have you looked at the instruction booklets that accompany a new phone, a new tool, or a new appliance? They are now usually written in many languages. Every time we pick one up it reminds us we live in a global culture.

Look at the various ethnic groups in our cities and towns. We hear foreign languages in the grocery stores and the gas stations.

These people may be our doctors or sales clerks, perhaps taxi drivers or hairdressers. I met a lady from Estonia this week who has a shop for alterations. People from China, India, Mexico, Iran, Korea, Saudi Arabia, Honduras, and elsewhere around the globe live among us, and they are becoming Americans.

The Great Commission says to "go," but we don't always need a passport. Because we are part of a global society, our missions work has become much easier to accomplish. The world literally has come to us. A Christian family can "go" in one sense without leaving their own country. How? By sharing the gospel with the diverse people of "all the world" (Mark 16:15) who live all around us. It is up to us to meet and get to know these people, to share the gospel with them.

Recently I had to hire a taxi from the airport. As I climbed in, I saw that my driver was of a different nationality than me. After I gave him my directions, I asked, "Tell me, what country are you from?"

"I'm from India. Do you know my country?" he replied.

"Actually, I do. I've been there a few times."

He went on to ask why I had been to India, and I told him I am a Christian and that I went to help Christian leaders in India build schools and hospitals.

"What city in India are you from?" was my next question to him.

"I'm from Mumbai. I have been over here for a year now." Sensing my openness, he paused and then asked, "Are all people here Christians?"

"No," I answered, a bit surprised by his assumption. "Our country was built on Christian principles, but not everyone is a Christian. Are you a Christian?"

"No, I'm a Hindu. I have always been a Hindu, but I want to know about Christianity. What can you tell me? Can you sit up here so we can talk?"

He stopped the taxi and I climbed in the front seat. What an interesting conversation. Right here in the United States I had the privilege of telling a man from India about God the Creator, the creation of humankind, and our sin; about God loving us so much that he sent messengers, and more messengers, and then two thousand years ago sent his only Son so that we could know how to have eternal life.

People like this man from India are all around us. They want to get to know us and hear about what it means to be a Christian. They have come to the United States for economic and educational opportunities, and some for personal freedom. Have you seen them? Have you spoken to them? Take the initiative and start conversations with them. Ask them questions about themselves and their countries. They will be totally surprised you want to listen.

Where is the world? It's as close as our neighbors, our grocery stores, our malls, and our taxis. Yes, the countries are still far away from us. And yet, thanks to our global society, we have the opportunity to "see" parts of the world and its people. We have the opportunity to see them as God sees them. And they have the opportunity to know us personally and hear our personal testimony about faith in Jesus Christ.

Your Family's World

As you see the people of the world and respond to them, so will your children. They will be with you during some of those times when you connect to people of other cultures. When they are not with you—when they are at school or at the gym or on the soccer field—they, too, will have opportunities to see the world and respond to it. You and your family members have a unique slice of the whole world, and together you have a unique way to reach that world.

WHAT YOU CAN DO TODAY AS A FAMILY

1. Take some time to describe your family's world—the people of various nationalities that you encounter routinely and those that are within a day's driving distance of your home.
2. List all the people you have encountered in the last week who you think are from another country by birth. Put a check mark next to those you might be able to befriend. Discuss ways you can show those checked on your list that you want to become friends.
3. List the various religions of the world you know something about. What countries have one of these as the prominent religion.
4. Get a world map and place it on a wall in or near your dining area. At mealtimes talk about the different countries and locate them. See who can locate the most countries.
5. Pray together that you can have a part in taking the message of Jesus Christ to these people in your world.

WHAT IS A
GREAT COMMISSION FAMILY?

He looked straight into my eyes as he answered my question about his childhood. "As I remember it, knowing and caring about people of other countries and cultures was always important in our family."

This young man, now in his thirties with a family of his own, recounted to me his lifelong interest in missions. Great memories, one after another, came to his mind as his story unfolded.

One Family's Story

> Mom and Dad took my two brothers and me to Mexico when I was only five. In one of those remote Mexican villages, I fell into a cactus plant. I had never seen a plant like that, and I will never forget it!

29

On a more serious note, I remember even at that young age seeing the poverty and wondering how the people lived with it. That memory has stayed with me throughout my life.

Another thing I remember is that we had people from other countries in our home all the time. The stories I heard, especially around the dinner table, were fascinating. I would sit there as long as our guests did, not wanting to miss anything.

Those times taught me at a very early age to accept cultural diversity. More importantly, they made me realize that not everyone in the world knows about Jesus, but they need to. When they learn about him, their lives are transformed.

I remember also the time my parents went on a trip to South America. I must have been about ten years old. When they returned, it was so exciting to hear them talk about what they experienced. I remember them telling about having to cross a big river in Paraguay in a dugout canoe. In the San Blas Islands they ate with an Indian family who served them fresh fish and bread cooked over an open fire. Dad said the kids there laughed and pointed at him because he was so tall compared to all the people on their island.

Those people knew about Jesus, Dad said, because a fisherman had learned about the Lord when he was working on a commercial fishing boat. He had come back home and taught the people of his village what he knew, which wasn't much. Mom and Dad spent the evening telling the people more about Jesus and explaining Scriptures to them. Dad said the people would have sat there all night listening to them, but he and Mom had to leave because foreigners were not allowed to stay all night on the island.

When I was a teen, I expressed a strong personal interest in learning Spanish. I know it was because my parents had taken me to Panama, Costa Rica, and Mexico. In the church services, I had heard songs I knew, but they were all in Spanish. I became curious as to how they were translated. Because language is such an important part of being in other countries and understanding what is going on there, my parents made arrangements for me to spend two months in Guatemala living with a native pastor and his family. I took the city bus to Spanish class every morning, and in the afternoon I spent time with the pastor's two sons. Because I was immersed in the culture, I learned a lot about

Guatemalans. I even learned to eat what they eat! That was a necessity, since McDonald's hadn't arrived in Guatemala!

That summer experience opened my eyes to many differences in our cultures. I discovered a lot of spiritism and animism in Guatemala, which was something new to me. As I saw the impact their religions had on the people, it made me see the value of my faith in Christ in a new way. It also impressed upon me the need to get the message of Jesus Christ to the people living there who did not know about him.

I remember something else from my childhood that made a lasting impression. One year my parents decided our family needed to take action when they discovered that our missionary friends in Mexico needed another car. Their old clunker couldn't make it anymore, Dad said. What did our family do? We talked about it, prayed about it, and bought a brand-new van and gave it to them! Everyone in the family got involved in raising the funds together.

From my earliest memories, our family was involved in the lives of people from other countries. We had a young man from Mexico at our home one Christmas. He couldn't understand why people weren't celebrating in the streets like they do in Mexico. Another time, when I was in high school, a student from Nicaragua came to live with us for a while. He was really interested in my school and our activities.

The most important fellow I met was a young man attending college in Houston. He had grown up in Monterrey, Mexico and was in the States studying to be a minister at a Bible college. He didn't know much English, just enough to get by. He lived in our home several summers. He was fun to be around, and we could tease him about his English and pull pranks on him. Later our family went to Monterrey and met his family. This man became a part of our family over the years. He is a pastor now, and we still stay in touch with him.

In retrospect, I would say that because of the choices my parents made and the opportunities they brought before us, everyone in our family came to understand that we needed to share our lives and our faith in Jesus with all kinds of people. Our family's experiences continue to influence my life today, also the way I am raising my own kids.

Another Family's Story

This family has three grown children who are missionaries. Each one is in full-time ministry. Here is the father's account of his family's choices and the results.

It was a conscious decision for my wife and me early in our marriage. We were in college then and members of the student volunteer group. The group challenged us to make a commitment. Here is what we signed in faith: *I will live my life, under God, for others rather than for myself. I will not drift through life but will do my utmost, by prayer, by investigation, by meditation and service, to discover that form and place in which I can become the largest use in the Kingdom of God. As I find it, I will follow it under the leadership of Jesus Christ, wheresoever it takes me, cost what it may.*

I shared this commitment with our children when they were young. They witnessed it in our ministry. We considered it important to let them know why we were giving our lives to the church, why a call to serve is among the highest calls one can possibly receive from the Lord, and why material gain was never a primary factor in our ventures.

We certainly cannot take credit for what God has done in the lives of our children, but I believe we have helped in the process.

A Family with a Heart for the World

Parents with a heart for the world—the heart of Jesus for the people of the world—will see to it that their children have a variety of experiences and opportunities that develop their knowledge and interest in missions. Here are some practical things to do that will be explained more fully in later chapters:

- Relationships with people of other cultures—people in the neighborhood, schools, stores, restaurants, and other parts of the community
- Relationships with missionaries and their families, both at church and in the home
- Family conversations focused on current events and world trends
- Family trips taken to experience other cultures and other countries
- Foreign language study
- Short-term missions experiences
- Sponsorship of children in other countries
- Talking about Jesus and giving money so others can learn about him
- Prayer times focused on missions, unreached people, and missionary needs
- Finding needs and planning to be a part of the solution
- A home environment that exemplifies a curiosity for a wide variety of people and their cultures
- People of other cultures as guests in the home
- Family involvement in missions conventions and conferences
- Parents' active involvement, so concepts are caught as well as taught

WHAT YOU CAN DO TODAY AS A FAMILY

1. Using the above list as a guide, write down any of these you are already doing to develop your family's heart for the world. Which should have the top priority? Is it currently your family's top priority?

2. How would you characterize your family today? Discuss what it would mean for your family to be a Great Commission family. Why is it important?
3. Decide one thing you can do as a family today or tomorrow as a step toward becoming a Great Commission family. Pray together that God will show you other ways to focus your future on this type of missions commitment. Take that step.

4

WHAT ARE GREAT COMMISSION KIDS?

It was Gary's turn to tuck the kids in bed. He needed to do it before he went over his sermon again for church in the morning. As he pulled the covers up around his six-year-old son's neck, he bent over to kiss him good night.

"Dad," Jeremy asked, "is Grandpa a pastor too?"

"Yes, Jeremy. Grandpa's a pastor."

"Dad, was his dad a pastor?" Jeremy continued.

"Yes, Jeremy. Your great-grandpa was a pastor as well."

A long silence followed. Then Jeremy groaned quietly, "Oh no."

It doesn't take long for children to understand that the Lord has plans for families and individuals who are committed to him. Jeremy's "Oh no" showed he was beginning to understand that there would be more to his life than playing games and shooting baskets. At age six he was realizing his heritage.

What are Great Commission kids? Children that have accepted the Lord as their Savior. Bible stories are engraved on their hearts from the lips of their parents. They see their dad and mom following Jesus and sharing their faith with others. These children are taught from the earliest age that God gave them an important purpose in the world. They see that they are connected to all people of the world because God loves them. They are kids in families that are living out the Great Commission. Their families make connecting to all kinds of people from every place in the world for the purpose of loving and sharing the love of Christ a priority in their lives. They have the joy of imitating their parents' concern for others.

Recognizing Great Commission Kids

Great Commission kids imitate what they learn from their parents and the church. They start witnessing without even knowing what *witness* means. Kids can be so uninhibited as they share with their friends what is important to them.

Laura once heard her four-year-old Daniel say to his friend next door, "Oh, Natalie, our God is an awesome God; he reigns." On another occasion he told Kimberly, "Jesus loves us and is watching over us." Still another time, he insisted on bringing home his Sunday school paper and giving it to another neighborhood friend.

This four-year-old was proclaiming the majesty of our Lord. He spoke of Jesus' love and concern, and he shared from God's Word. Obviously he enjoyed learning about Jesus and wanted to share that joy with others.

Heather was five years old and excited about going to vacation Bible school. She told her new friend, Becky, who lived two doors down, about it and invited her to go along. Becky

36

was excited, because she had never been to church. On the third day, the teacher was telling the children that Jesus came to save them and they could be in the family of God. "Becky," Heather asked, "would you like to ask Jesus to be your Savior? If you will, then God will be your heavenly Father too." When Becky said yes, Heather and Becky knelt together to pray. The teacher slipped over and helped Becky with her prayer of repentance. Heather and Becky rushed home to tell their mothers that Becky made that commitment. They remained close friends going to church together until Becky's family moved away.

Great Commission kids develop behaviors that can become lifelong habits in their lives. Here are a few.

Giving and Sharing Money and Resources

Being disciplined, responsible, focused, and intense is not normal for a teenager. But that's Peter. He has a deep sense of financial responsibility and has learned the joy of giving. When a need is brought to his attention, Peter responds. Through family discussions of politics, world events, and global concepts and a family lifestyle of responding to the needs of others in love, he has caught on to the joy of giving and sharing.

Exhibiting a Caring and Sensitive Spirit

Sue and her family took compassion on a pregnant Muslim girl from Jordan. It just seemed right, since the girl was here in the United States without a husband, a home, or anyone to care for her. Sue convinced her family to take care of the young woman until her little girl was born and she was able to return to her own country. Sue's caring and sensitive spirit led her family to show the love of Christ in a practical way.

Showing Lively Interest in Others

Kristen loves Hispanic people. She likes to speak Spanish. Anytime she can befriend and help a Hispanic person, she does. She has gone to Mexico on eight short-term teen missions trips to teach vacation Bible school. "I think the Lord especially put Mexico in my heart. Responding to their needs is important to me."

But it's not just Mexico. Kristen is presently in India working for the India Gospel League. She travels to various villages, documenting the work that is taking place, taking pictures, and updating communication pieces. She will graduate from Taylor University with a major in communications and a minor in marketing and is ready to go into full-time work for the Lord.

Seeing Opportunities and Responding

Chris works in inner city Chicago—by choice. When he was younger, his parents took his entire family to Haiti, Ecuador, and Peru. He saw poverty and the need for Christ. When he visited Chicago, it was natural for him to see an opportunity in the inner city and respond. "Chicago is where I'm supposed to be now, and I want to be where the Lord wants me to be."

Enjoying New Cultures, New Languages, and New Places

It is not unusual for a sixteen-year-old boy to want to explore, but it is unusual for one to want to explore the world anywhere, anytime. That is Andrew. Even as a five-year-old boy, he told his dad, "I'm just glad to be anywhere that God has made." He has already been to seven countries, and he plans to include Moscow in his future trips. He also wants to go to India. His father has been there several times. Having heard his father's stories, Andrew has a desire in his heart to see for himself this strange and distant world.

Seeing and Seizing Challenges

Erin's eyes are always busy. She sees adventure, and wherever she looks she has compassion on those in need. When she sees a family at church struggling to get their three children out of the car, she helps. When she sees a non-English speaker at school, she offers to tutor. Her time and effort are not as important as responding to what the Lord is showing her. Her purpose is to help people—wherever, whenever, whoever.

Desiring to Explore the World

Going to Africa is on Sarah's agenda for the future. Her parents took her to three countries when she was in high school. She has spent six weeks in India working with outcastes and a summer with an evangelistic team in Europe. Her interest is to explore the world for the purpose of seeing how she can serve and to be faithful in every opportunity. God is showing her his world and what she can do for him.

Developing Great Commission Kids through the Five Senses

How do Great Commission kids develop these behaviors? They have parents who are determined to model and help develop those behaviors. All parents know the special joy that comes to them as they teach their children to dress themselves, enjoy books, and learn to ride a tricycle and a bicycle. An even greater parenting joy comes in Great Commission families—to teach children about the world God created and its diversity.

Using the five senses as training tools, parents can lead their children to develop a global vision and global consciousness.

Training the Eyes

The eyes are the earliest tools available to parents for training children to see the world as God would have them see it. Every young child likes stories. Colorful storybooks about children from other lands help toddlers and elementary school children see that not everybody is like them. Showing young children pictures of different races and strange clothing helps them understand and accept these differences.

Television programs and videos can be even more visually stimulating than books. World maps on bedroom walls and inexpensive globes enable children to locate the places they see on television. Knowing the location of each of the continents, the United States, and the children's and parents' hometowns adds context. When the TV news or newspapers carry conversations about faraway places such as China and Korea, children can learn to find those places on the map or globe and pray for the people who live there. Visual exposure goes a long way in developing a sense of the world and children's place in it.

Developing Hearing

Hearing words and phrases from foreign languages at an early age helps children understand the diversity and complexity of God's creation. Parents can use words from other languages as basic instructions around the home. Calling the family to the dinner table with "vamos a comer" is an example. Even if children don't progress far in the use of such words or phrases, they've begun the process of learning multiple languages.

In multicultural America, children hear English spoken with many different accents. These are opportunities to talk about the speakers—people who obviously have different places of origin. On these occasions, parents can conjecture with their children on what it may be like to leave home and country and all that is familiar and why people would do so—out of economic necessity, vocation, personal interest, or a "calling" in the Christian sense of that word.

Interviews with persons from other cultures and countries will give children opportunities to listen. Through these activities, they can develop the relational skill of listening closely and responding with appropriate questions. During or after an interview, depending on the circumstances, the one question that should always be asked and answered is whether the person interviewed has ever heard of Jesus Christ.

Using Touch

If their eyes see it, children want to touch it. Because young children get used to hearing "Don't touch," parents have a wonderful opportunity to teach them about the world by using touch as a tool.

Parents can bring items from other cultures to their children and let them touch and examine, feel various textures, and run their fingertips over them. The conversations begin simply by parents asking how these things feel and why.

Displaying inexpensive artifacts from other countries in the home is a good way to help develop the sense of touch. Parents can find such artifacts in stores like Hobby Lobby, Bombay Company, World Market, and Pier One Imports. These items also can be found in missions displays at church. As children are invited to touch these items, parents can talk about how they were made, what country they were made in, the raw materials used in construction and why, who made the items and why, how much time was involved in the making, and how the items came to be here. More questions will follow. How much do these items cost to purchase, and how much money did the person who made them receive? What will that amount of money buy for a person in the country where the item was made?

Bibles from other countries are wonderful items to touch and handle and discuss. Do all the people who can read this Bible's language know about Jesus? Why or why not? How many of the people who speak the language of this Bible can read its contents? Do they all have Bibles, or only some of them? Why?

Touching people of other races and nationalities is important too. Children's initial shyness to touch someone who is "different" from them can be replaced by joy, and a personal connection can be made that might otherwise not be possible. More ideas and suggestions for touching people are included in later chapters as we talk about missionaries and native pastors visiting the home, opportunities for hosting a foreign student, and short-term mission experiences.

Discovering Smell and Taste

Smells and tastes can excite children and teach them a great deal about other cultures. As parents make a practice of going to various ethnic restaurants, children become accustomed to smelling and tasting a diversity of foods. These restaurants typically have table servers or cooks who are native to the featured country. They may have an accent or not even know English all that well, so there's an added opportunity for learning through sight and sound and even touch.

Heather's Story

Heather learned about people of other cultures through her family experiences in ethnic restaurants. "My parents especially liked to take us to the Star of Siam, a Thai restaurant in our city. I was in junior high at that time, and I was intrigued with foreign culture. Dad knew that, so before we went there the first time he showed us on the map where Thailand is located and how far it is from our home.

"Our waiter was a young man from Thailand. We had a good time talking with him as he served us. That, plus the good food, made me want to return. After that first visit, he seemed to look forward to our coming to the restaurant. Each visit we enjoyed talking with him further and asking questions about his country.

"After several visits my sister and I decided to go there just to see our friend and talk with him. We talked about all kinds of things. He learned what Christmas meant to us, because we took the time to talk to him about Jesus. He even sent us Christmas cards for years until we finally lost touch with him."

Developing Great Commission Kids through Family Habits

Great Commission kids have habits that shape their lives and enlarge their hearts. These habits are the result of choices the parents made to mold the lives of their children.

The Habit of Scripture Memorization

Great Commission families develop the habit of memorizing Scripture. Kids can be taught Bible verses at home at every age, beginning at about age three. Begin with simple Scriptures such as 1 John 4:16—"God is love"; Genesis 1:1—"In the beginning God created the heavens and the earth"; and parts of John 3:16 a bit at a time—"For God so loved the world that he gave his one and only Son, that whoever believes in him shall not perish but have eternal life."

By the age of eight, most children can memorize and comprehend the meaning of Matthew 28:19–20 and Mark 16:15.

Other important verses are Philippians 4:4, Psalm 118:24, and John 3:3. At this age they can memorize the chapter and verse numbers of the Scriptures.

Many other Scriptures can be selected as children's memory skills and ages advance to challenge them in their worldview, to help them see other people through the eyes of Jesus Christ, to develop a servant heart, to be equipped to share the gospel, and to grow as disciples. A list of some key Scriptures appears at the end of this chapter.

The Habit of Prayer

Praying for other people is a priority for Great Commission kids. As parents pray on a daily basis with children, they instill in children love and care about the needs of people all over the world. Praying together Psalm 67:2—"that your ways may be known on earth, your salvation among all nations"—brings out the relevance of the Scriptures to the concerns family members bring to prayer times.

Since everyone's life is busy but everyone needs to eat, you might make your prayer time right before or after your evening meal. Some days it may be hurried, but other days you could have more time to pray. Use the front page of the newspaper to initiate prayer time. Do what you can when you can, but make it a priority.

How do you begin a habit of family prayer for the people of the world? It can begin as simply as spinning a globe. Using a child's finger to stop the globe, you can pray right then for that particular country. The book *Operation World* by Patrick Johnstone will give you valuable information about nations and peoples as well as their spiritual needs. You can look up a particular country and find out how many Christians and how many non-Christians live there, what religions are practiced there, and if there is persecution or freedom. If your children have developed curiosity for learning new things, it will be time well spent to look up different countries and discuss information about our world and how Christ might see it.

WHAT YOU CAN DO TODAY AS A FAMILY

1. Individually discuss your children's relationship with the Lord. If they have not made a commitment to Jesus Christ as their Savior, this is the time to help them make that commitment. If they have already accepted Christ, you will want to review that time and emphasize the importance that decision has in making them children of God.

2. Talk to your children about the kind of people they would like to be—now and when they are adults. Ask them to describe behaviors, habits, and attitudes they would like to have.

3. If you haven't purchased a globe or a wall map, do so. If you have, talk about how you can begin to use it.

4. Discuss family prayer time, and choose someone to be in charge each week.

5. Start a Scripture memory system. You might want to discuss rewards for a certain number of Scriptures memorized. Rewards can be anything from a computer-generated certificate to cash or special privileges.

Selected Missions Scriptures

Following is a short list of suggested Scriptures for memorization. As you read your Bible or hear messages at church, add to this list.

"He will save his people from their sins" (Matt. 1:21).

"Ask the Lord of the harvest, therefore, to send out workers" (Matt. 9:38).

"Therefore go and make disciples of all nations, baptizing them in the name of the Father and of the Son and of the Holy Spirit . . ." (Matt. 28:19–20).

"Go into all the world and preach the good news to all creation" (Mark 16:15).

"The harvest is plentiful, but the workers are few" (Luke 10:2).

"Go out to the roads and country lanes and make them come in so that my house will be full" (Luke 14:23).

"Repentance and forgiveness of sins will be preached in his name to all nations" (Luke 24:47).

"For God so loved the world that he gave his one and only Son, that whoever believes in him shall not perish but have eternal life" (John 3:16).

"Whoever believes in the Son has eternal life, but whoever rejects the Son will not see life" (John 3:36).

"Open your eyes and look at the fields! They are ripe for harvest" (John 4:35).

"We know that this man really is the Savior of the world" (John 4:42).

"I am the way and the truth and the life. No one comes to the Father except through me" (John 14:6).

"You did not choose me, but I chose you and appointed you to go and bear fruit" (John 15:16).

"As the Father has sent me, I am sending you" (John 20:21).

"But you will receive power when the Holy Spirit comes on you; and you will be my witnesses" (Acts 1:8).

"I am not ashamed of the gospel, because it is the power of God for the salvation of everyone who believes" (Rom. 1:16).

"For all have sinned and fall short of the glory of God" (Rom. 3:23).

"For the wages of sin is death, but the gift of God is eternal life in Christ Jesus our Lord" (Rom. 6:23).

"Everyone who calls on the name of the Lord will be saved" (Rom. 10:13).

"How, then, can they call on the one they have not believed in? And how can they believe in the one of whom they have not heard? And how can they hear without someone preaching to them? And how can they preach unless they are sent?" (Rom. 10:14–15).

"The god of this age has blinded the minds of unbelievers, so that they cannot see the light of the gospel of the glory of Christ, who is the image of God" (2 Cor. 4:4).

"I can do everything through him who gives me strength" (Phil. 4:13).

"All over the world this gospel is bearing fruit and growing, just as it has been doing among you since the day you heard it and understood God's grace in all its truth" (Col. 1:6).

"This is the gospel that you heard and that has been proclaimed to every creature under heaven" (Col. 1:23).

"For the grace of God that brings salvation has appeared to all men" (Titus 2:11).

"Never will I leave you; never will I forsake you" (Heb. 13:5).

"But if serving the LORD seems undesirable to you, then choose for yourselves this day whom you will serve. . . . But as for me and my household, we will serve the LORD" (Josh. 24:15).

"The Lord does not look at the things man looks at. Man looks at the outward appearance, but the LORD looks at the heart" (1 Sam. 16:7).

"All the ends of the earth will remember and turn to the LORD, and all the families of the nations will bow down before him" (Ps. 22:27).

"Commit your way to the LORD; trust in him and he will do this" (Ps. 37:5).

"That your ways may be known on earth, your salvation among all nations" (Ps. 67:2).

"Then I heard the voice of the LORD saying, 'Whom shall I send? And who will go for us?'" (Isa. 6:8).

"I will also make you a light for the Gentiles, that you may bring my salvation to the ends of the earth" (Isa. 49:6).

"The LORD will lay bare his holy arm in the sight of all the nations, and all the ends of the earth will see the salvation of our God" (Isa. 52:10).

Let's Have a Party!

Invite me to a party and I'll be there. Mention the word *party* to my kids and they want to know when, where, and who. We are ready. The thought of a party always lights up our eyes and expectations.

Once I threw a Mexican fiesta. The invitations stated that those invited were to come dressed in anything they could find that looked Mexican. Don a sombrero. Sport a bold Mexican shirt. Twirl in a flamenco skirt. Brush up on those Spanish phrases because we were going to try out every Spanish word we knew on each other. This event was to be an authentic "south of the border" party.

This fiesta called for decorations—lots of them. The house was bedecked with streamers, candles, Mexican vases, pictures, papier-mâché dolls, and everything else we could imagine that might represent Mexico. We had the spirit of Mexico. Turn up the Latin music. Break out those Spanish greetings. Vamanos!

Our friends came expecting tacos, burritos, quesadillas, chimichangas, frijoles, and salsa, and they got them. They were

49

expecting Mexican music, and it surrounded them. They were expecting Spanish phrases, and they heard them. We brushed up on some Spanish greetings. Our "Buenos noches," "pase adelante," and "mi casa es tuya" might not have had the right accent, but they gave the evening the atmosphere we wanted. Besides the "Buenos noches," some of our guests even got as far as "Donde vive ahora?" Spirits were high. Their laughter convinced me that they were all having a good time. If learning about the culture and lifestyle of others could be this much fun, then bring it on.

But there was more. I had invited my friend from Mexico. He blended in, but it was easy to tell that he was the true Mexican among us. He had been to the States more times than he could remember, so he was comfortable with us and the party idea. My husband and I had met Enrique in 1964 when we were planning our first trip to Mexico. He had been our guide on that first trip, and a bond was formed. Our friendship had blossomed over the years, and he became as special to us as if he were one of our sons.

Parties to Learn

The learning portion of our party started with a simple question. "Enrique, tell us how weddings are done in Mexico." Then came a flood of other questions. "Are most Mexicans Catholic?" "What are the schools like?" "Do you take siestas every day?" "What is the story about the Virgin of Guadalupe?" "How many different Mexican tribes are there?" "Does each tribe speak a different language?" "What is the currency?" "Why do so many Mexican people cross the border into our country?" Questions popped up from everywhere.

A map of Mexico had been tacked on the wall. Enrique used it as he answered questions. Our pictures of Mexico City,

Taxco, Tampico, Chihuahua, and Pueblo as well as a snapshot of Enrique's family with eleven brothers and sisters and his parents added to the stories.

Enrique told us about the churches in Mexico and what his church was like. He shared that he had learned about Jesus Christ through missionaries. A family had moved to Saltillo to teach in a Bible school and tell people in the villages of that area about the Christian faith. Few people in those villages had ever heard the good news of Jesus Christ. The missionaries led Enrique's family to the Lord. They introduced whole communities and villages to the gospel and guided them in the Christian faith.

At this point one of our better Spanish speakers at the party read the Twenty-third Psalm in Spanish. Enrique interpreted verse by verse. God's Word sounded so different and yet still familiar.

The missions Bible school in Saltillo trained the young people of Mexico to be pastors and teachers. La Buena Tierra was running to capacity when Enrique enrolled. There his faith in Christ was established, and he made his commitment to become a minister of the gospel. Christian missions and missionaries had made a powerful impact on his life. Now he was influencing our guests at the party. The flame of the gospel those missionaries had shared with him was being passed on right here among us.

The party tantalized us all to learn more about Mexico and the Mexican people. One of my son's friends told me as he was leaving, "If this is a part of missions, then missions is fun. I want to learn more."

Okay, maybe you don't have a friend like Enrique, but people from other countries in your neighborhood could be the spark for your party even if they don't yet know Christ. They could be waiting for a chance like this to tell about their country, their family back home, and their culture. Throw your party. Let them share. This could be your chance to introduce them to Christ and bring missions right in your front door.

In Your Own Backyard

Here's another party approach. How about that family from India down the block, the Vietnamese couple you met at parents' night at school, or perhaps another foreign-born family you have been introduced to? Ask them over for dinner or dessert and learn about each other some evening. Plan a game such as "Twenty Questions" where you can bring up the differences and similarities in families, countries, concepts, and traditions. Create an exciting evening of learning about each other.

Fit these kinds of parties into your family's lifestyle. They can be your family's way of doing missions, of doing evangelism, and of learning about cultures and people. They can be your way of training your kids to see the world through the eyes of Christ.

Take the next step by challenging your church to give "mission" parties. Enlarge what you have done at home to become an outreach for the whole church. You can make missions exciting for the whole congregation as you challenge church people to expand their thinking, their concepts of how to reach out to others, and their understanding of the world that now surrounds us.

Beyond Your Backyard

If you're going to take this party thing seriously, you'll want to look further than your backyard and your personal friends. Are there ethnic festivals in your area? If your city has a Greek festival, it will be an opportunity to learn about Greece and its people.

Before you go, give your kids a list of things to look for during the festival or discuss it before you go depending on their age. During the festival, talk about how things are different and can be exciting. You might have them take along a notebook and write down things they see that are different or that they want to learn more about. What is the language? Where is Greece? What do Greek people look like? How do they dress? What do they eat? How is their food different than ours? Enjoy the party, and let the questions roll. You can fill in the gaps on other aspects of Greek culture later at home.

Find out about other local festivals. Oktoberfest is sponsored by those who want to share their German heritage. Once again, you can get ready for the event with questions to be answered and things to look for.

What do nearby cities have to offer? Do some research and find out what is going on in the major ethnic communities within a day's drive of your area. Detroit's Middle Eastern communities offer lots of opportunities to participate in their activities and mix with the people. Check into the cultural celebrations in other big cities.

Rubbing shoulders with people of other nationalities is one of the best ways to realize the numerous differences in our cultures. America is blessed with many different ethnic groups that provide fantastic opportunities to enhance our vision of the world.

Check Your Understandings

After a party, take time to evaluate your experiences. Some points you might want to discuss in a family meeting are:

- What did you learn about the people's culture and their country?
- How much do they know about Jesus Christ?
- What is their concept of Christianity?
- How can we help them know Christ as their Savior?
- How many people live in their country?
- What is their religion?
- Do we know any missionaries there?
- What should we do next?

You are redefining the word *missions* in the context of your children's understanding and abilities. You are giving it a definition that has significant meaning for them, and you are building their desire to be involved in missions. You are establishing a foundation for missions on which your children can build their lives and their future with Christ. You are also helping them understand the value of their own heritage—that someone sometime brought the gospel to your family.

Besides all that, it's fun.

WHAT YOU CAN DO TODAY AS A FAMILY

1. Select a culture that you can use as a theme for a party.
2. Identify a friend or representative of that culture who you could ask to help you plan the party and attend.
3. Enlist your kids in planning decorations and refreshments and include their ideas about whom to invite.
4. Pray with your kids for the party.
5. Throw the party and have fun. Enjoy the new culture.

Afterward, discuss the differences with your kids and why it is so important for everyone to know Jesus Christ.

ARE MISSIONARIES
REAL PEOPLE?

I'm standing at the front door waiting. The toys are picked up. The skates and bicycles are stashed in the garage. My kids have on clean shirts and their hair is combed. Dinner is ready. What will this evening be like? I look at my boys—they are four, six, and ten years old. Wonderful ages. The boys think this special dinner is for our guests, the visiting missionaries at our church. It isn't. It's for the boys to meet these missionaries. To find out what they are like. To discover what they do. To ask about life as missionaries living in Kenya, Africa.

"Go out and welcome our guests, boys. Help them with their luggage. Carry it in for them."

The LaFonts are a friendly couple. She is talking with the boys. He is helping the youngest find something to carry. My oldest, who is giving up his room for the night, is their guide, showing them the room where they will be staying. This has the possibility of a great evening and a special experience for my kids.

I get dinner on the table while my husband and boys show them around. It isn't long before we are seated at the dining room table. Our conversation is friendly, and then it turns a corner when our youngest son asks, "Mr. LaFont, where is Kenya? Is it in Africa?" He's the most inquisitive of the boys. Frank and Margaret LaFont are great at responding to the string of questions that follow. What lively conversation ensued, punctuated with stories of the jungle and lions, zebras, and elephants!

The more serious questions come next—about the people, the huts, and the witch doctors. The LaFonts explain that their job is to teach the African people about the one true God. They tell stories of how the gospel of Jesus Christ changes the lives of the people.

My boys are wide-eyed as they begin to understand what the LaFonts do, what missionaries do. They see that missionaries are real people like them, and like their mom and dad. They discover that missionaries have children too. The LaFont kids go to boarding school in Africa. What's that? It's a whole new concept for my boys compared to living in Kansas and attending grade school a few blocks from home.

After dinner comes picture time. We want to make this evening a special memory for everyone. The camera comes out, and my husband lines up the boys with the LaFonts. Click! Another one with dad in the picture. Click! We know what those pictures will show us when they are developed. What we don't know is what the lives of our boys will show us when they are developed, but this evening will be a part of it.

Before the boys' bedtime, we form a circle with our guests. Holding hands, each one of us prays. The prayers of the boys are precious. In their prayer with their heavenly Father, each injects something he just learned that night from the earlier conversation.

That evening was repeated in our home many times with many different missionaries. The visitors came from as far away as Australia, Bangladesh, Egypt, and Panama and as close as Mexico. Lively conversations. Great insights and challenges for our boys.

Whenever my boys heard people pray " . . . and Lord, bless the missionaries around the world," they'd whispered to me, "Don't they know their names?" Our family did.

Making Missionary Memories with Your Children

What can you do to help your children see missionaries as real people? You can take your children to missions conferences. You can read them stories about missionaries. You can read missionaries' newsletters together as a family. There's no substitute, however, for bringing missionaries into your home. Here are some ideas for making those visits memorable.

When you know you are going to have missionaries in your home, plan the visit in advance with your children's input. Have your children buy or make a gift for each of your guests. Tell them this gesture is often a cultural requirement in many countries. It's a good idea in our culture too. A good time for your children to give the guests these gifts is at the dinner table after the plates are cleared away.

You might have your children plan a short program. It could include a song, the reciting of some favorite Scripture verses the children have memorized, or even a play your children have prepared. Your guests will love whatever you do, and your children will enjoy their participation in the evening.

If your children are in their teens, they may be more interested in preparing a list of questions to ask the missionaries about teenagers in their country. They are sure to want to know if their teenagers can drive a car, plus what it is like to drive in their country. They may want to know if they have a high school close to where they live, or if they have to go to a boarding school. What happens when it is time to go to college? Do they go to college in the country or come back to the United States? If they come back here, do they stay with their grandparents? It wouldn't take much for your teenagers to have a barrage of questions about teenage life in another country.

Here's more. Not long after their visit, write these missionary friends a letter from the entire family. Send them copies of the photos you took with them. Send them one of your family photos, too, and ask for one of theirs. Keep them in your daily family prayers, reminding the children of the needs they shared when they were with you.

Keep the communication up to date so the friendship can develop. Keep in touch by e-mail. Send the family members small gifts at Christmas. Post their letters on your bulletin board or refrigerator. Do whatever you can to fan the flame and keep the memories alive. And do whatever you can to have those missionaries back in your home for another visit in the future.

Keeping It Vital

I have an important photo album in my house. My boys are grown now, with families of their own, and I keep the album where they can find it when they come to visit. It's an album of the pictures of those nights, of the boys posing with the many missionaries we hosted. There's the photo of the LaFonts and our boys. There they are a few years later with the Shottons from Mexico and the Swarts from Australia. Those photos of the Lopezes from Nicaragua are precious! Page after page of precious memories.

The boys still like to pull out that album and look again at those photos. What is especially rewarding to me is listening to my sons explain the pictures to their children: "Look at this one. Their kids went to a boarding school. See this couple? They came upon a lion one day when they were walking to church." Their explanations and memories are not the same as mine because they were young, but the theme is the same—missionaries are real people.

WHAT YOU CAN DO TODAY AS A FAMILY

1. Ask your pastor or missions pastor when missionaries are scheduled to visit. Ask if you can possibly have them as your guests for lunch or an evening.
2. Buy a photo album to fill it with photos from the missionary visits you plan to have.
3. Send birthday and Christmas cards to the missionaries your children have met, and send them to those you want to have in your home sometime in the future.
4. Your children can pinpoint on your family's world map the countries where your missionary friends live and work.
5. Talk about missionaries at the dinner table, sharing any recent news you've heard. Remind your children of the evenings with those missionaries and brainstorm future visits.
6. Remember these missionaries in your family prayers.

7

FUN AND GAMES

"Marty, I've got an idea. You like to play games, don't you?" Nancy said to her ten-year-old son. "How would you like to play 'Who Wants to Be a Millionaire'?"

"Wow, Mom. That would be cool. I'd really like that. Maybe I could make a million. When can we do that?" She had Marty's full attention.

"Marty, this is what I've been thinking. We could plan a special game night and invite some of your friends from the church. We'll give everyone special things to study to be ready for the game. The theme of the game will be places around the world and what is being done to reach people for Jesus. We have money for prizes, too, but it won't be a million. How would you like that?"

"Sounds cool, Mom. I'd like that. Could we invite Eddie and Bryson and Michael and . . . wow. We could invite lots of people and make it a really big game. Let's do it, Mom."

Games are a creative way to bring missions and the Great Commission into your lives. Here are some ideas you can adapt for your kids and their friends. They will love you for it, and the word will get out around your community about the innovative and fun things you are doing.

"Who Wants to Be a Millionaire?"

Because of the popularity of this game as a result of the television show, there is usually an immediate interest in playing it. If you place the emphasis on missions, you will have a winner.

1. *Gather information on the missionaries your church supports.* You need their names, children, locations, ministry purposes, sending organizations, how long your church has supported them, their home base, and anything else pertinent to their particular ministries. Prepare this information to give to the contestants as background for the game.

2. *Gather information on the mission organizations your church supports.* What do they do? Where do they work? Where are the headquarters? How many full-time and part-time workers do they have? How many years have they been with the organization? How much does your church give to them annually and for how long? Add this information to the folder of information you are preparing for the contestants.

3. *Choose one or two books of missions stories.* Choose those that show the excitement, the direction from the Lord, and the problems and joys of mission work. My first book, *Climb Another Mountain,* may be useful. You might also consider *Peace Child* by Don Richardson. Let your contestants know that some of your questions will come from these books.

4. *Determine the prize amounts.* There are many options here. Choose your "million-dollar" figure, and work from there. You could have $28 as the "million" by starting with $1, then $2, then $4, and then multiples of four up to $28. Or you

could start with $5, $10, and so on. The cash prize could go to the winner, or better yet it could be given to the winner to designate to a missions project of his choice.

5. *Write "quick draw" questions and prize questions with four possible answers to each one.* The quick-draw questions are used to determine the contestant. From there, organize your questions to increase in difficulty up to the one for the "million-dollar" prize.

6. *Set a date and time for the game, and inform those who will attend of the rules.* Prepare a folder of information for each contestant to study in preparation for the game. You may want to invite entire families and ask them to designate one family member as their contestant.

7. *Plan your game area along the lines of the setup used on TV.* You need a contestant's chair, quizmaster's chair, and places for the audience. You might want to add music and lights to help create excitement. And of course you will need a quizmaster and someone to dispense the prize money.

8. *Build excitement among contestants in the weeks and days preceding the game.* Remind the contestants that they need to study the materials you've provided, read the book or books you've indicated in order to qualify as a participant. Two weeks should give them enough time to prepare and time for the enthusiasm to grow.

9. *Prepare a "Who Wants to Be a Millionaire?" sign for the day of the game, to add to the excitement.*

10. *The game itself proceeds as follows*: A quick-draw question is asked. The first contestant is chosen. That person moves to the "hot seat." As the contestant answers the first question, and then the second, moving on higher in the prize money, the excitement grows. Eventually the contestant misses a question, steps down, and is awarded his prize money. The next contestant then settles in the chair, and the game begins again.

As the money you have allotted diminishes, announce that there will only be three more contestants so you won't disappoint anyone or have to quickly come up with more money.

Since all of the questions are about missions, everyone, including the audience, learns about missions. You can be sure that your kids will want to repeat this memorable experience. It's a fun way to learn about missions.

Other Game Shows

Other game shows can be adapted as well. Watch *Jeopardy* or *Wheel of Fortune* for a couple of nights on TV, and then work out your plan to turn these games into missions games. The prizes can be items such as a trip, an item donated by a friend, or funds earmarked for a short-term missions experience.

Board Games

Missionary Conquest is a great board game. It is similar to Monopoly or Risk. It should be available at your local Christian bookstore, or the store manager can order it for you. The object of the game is to establish missions ministries in countries throughout the world and to earn "blessing points." You win by how many blessings you receive as you play, not, as in other board games, by how much wealth you have accumulated. That is a new and difficult concept for our American mentality.

Look at the board games you have in your home. Perhaps you will be able to modify one to develop into a missions game. If you do, let me know about it!

It's going to be a toss-up to see who learns the most—the kids or the parents. I have discovered that I learn a great deal when I am in charge of a project. We all seem to learn more if there is a reason to learn. Watch out! As you lead your kids to become Great Commission kids, you become Great Commission disciples of the Lord.

WHAT YOU CAN DO AS A FAMILY

1. Talk over the idea of having parties and playing missions games with your family. Decide which TV and board games you would like to use.
2. Watch the TV game shows you have chosen at least two times, with a notepad in hand to catch the content, procedures, and other information you'll need for your version.
3. Read the "How to Play" directions of the board games you have chosen and write down a complete set of your revised game instructions.
4. Plan your game night. Choose the place, time, guests, procedures, and prizes. (You may want to bring a Sunday school class or other group into your planning and enlist the help of that leader.)
5. Pray as a family about the upcoming party.
6. After the game night, discuss what each one learned about missions. Plan the next game night.

You've Got Mail

I've got a letter. Mom, I've got a letter," your son cries out as he rushes in the door. You see the excitement on his face as he tears open the letter. "It's from India. He wrote me a letter. He must have gotten mine. Mom, let's see what he says." Getting a letter from a friend is always exciting and even more so if it is from overseas.

Your child can develop relationships that broaden his world perspective by using the avenues available today in correspondence. E-mail is so simple and quick. It can be quite short, which is sometimes more welcome than other forms of correspondence. Whether you use the conventional mail service or e-mail, getting and sending letters or messages to others is a wonderful way to expand your children's world.

Getting Started

Some basic ingredients are important in the correspondence experience. First, decide how many correspondents you want your children to have. Next, decide who the correspondents will be. Start at your local church by getting information on the missionaries your church supports. Do they have children? If so, what are their ages? Your children will probably enjoy writing to these children, and if the missionary children are away in a boarding school, they will welcome the letters even more. Of course, finding a letter in the mailbox with a foreign stamp on it is a special joy for children. Collecting the stamps can be fun too.

Besides U.S. missionaries, your church also might sponsor national Christian leaders in other countries. Inquire about these leaders' children, and find out how correspondence can be developed. Is your family sponsoring a child in a foreign country? How often do you send support checks? Do you write letters? That child would enjoy receiving correspondence from your child.

After you've determined who your children's correspondents will be, it's time for geography lessons with a purpose. Use your world map or globe to locate the country and possibly the city where each of your children's correspondents are, marking the locations with a pin or a marker. Have discussion about that region of the world. Is it in the 10/40 Window? What are the major religions? Are there many Christians? What countries are nearby? What is the climate there, and how does it affect people's lifestyles? Here is where the book *Operation World* will come in handy again.

Find out if regular correspondence back and forth more than once or twice a year is possible. Sometimes it is difficult to receive regular messages in return, so your children will have to understand that. Sometimes you may need to provide funds for return postage, which is much higher in most other countries, where even the cost of a stamp can become a problem.

Set up a system for keeping track of correspondence. Get a scrapbook to save letters and envelopes that come in the mail. If the correspondence is via e-mail, set up a special directory for this mail.

What to Say

When they begin correspondence, the first thing your children should write about is who they are and why they are writing. Other topics: family members, school, pets, neighbors, hobbies, vacations, church activities, the weather, music lessons, and extracurricular activities. Write about your church. Tell them what church you go to, what happens at your church, and what you like best. Your children also can send their pictures or the whole family's picture, either printed or in an e-mail.

Coach your children on asking good questions. They should ask the correspondent about where he or she lives, what their house is like, what the food is like, what school is like, what people wear in that country, and any prayer needs. They can ask for a photo too.

You'll think of more things you can do after the initial correspondence. How about sending stickers, mailing audio or video messages and songs, including photos of building snowmen or planting a garden, exchanging postcards of your cities, or sharing family or cultural stories?

Children might enjoy sending and receiving jigsaw puzzle letters. You can cut the letter into shapes for special days or seasons, for example, birthday cakes, Valentine hearts, Christmas trees or bells, and Easter crosses. Artwork and special pictures that have been made for your friends are always appreciated.

Sometimes these childhood correspondence arrangements develop into precious friendships. At the very least, they create a lively interest in another country and the people who live there.

Adding Joy

With some encouragement from you, your children can clip interesting articles from newspapers or magazines to send. An added excitement is helping your children remember and honor their new friend's birthday, Christmas, and other important holidays. An easy way to help your children remember these special dates is to have them scheduled on a calendar. If you can, plan to send a surprise periodically. For example, you could send a birthday party in a box. Now who wouldn't like that?

Making the most of the correspondence experience involves sharing information with others. Your children can report on their mail at your family's dinnertime and share any pictures they receive. They can also take letters to school or use the information in them for school reports.

Watching your children developing these relationships will be rewarding and exciting for you. They can begin to develop a servant heart and a greater understanding of the world in which they live. These relationships can last a lifetime. We cannot know where the Lord will take this effort and how it will be multiplied, but we do know God will use it.

WHAT YOU CAN DO TODAY AS A FAMILY

1. Contact your church or mission board to research missionary families with children. Get e-mail and postal addresses.

2. Discuss the information with your children and talk about developing relationships. Make decisions you all can embrace.
3. Locate the country or countries of correspondents on a world map.
4. Provide your children with necessary equipment and postage or Internet access for e-mail.
5. When mail arrives, post it on the refrigerator or a special place of prominence. Talk about it at your dinner table.

DEVELOPING JESUS' VISION

Having 20/20 vision has not been one of my privileges; I have worn glasses since the fifth grade. My vision has changed over the years, but unfortunately not for the better. When you reach your forties, you will probably hear the word *bifocals*. The good news for all of us is that we don't need bifocals to see the world through the eyes of Christ.

When I take someone to visit a foreign country, I always tell them, "Now is the time to learn to see through the eyes of Jesus Christ." I usually get the quizzical look I expect, so I continue and explain what I mean. "Just suppose Jesus is walking alongside us. He is one of us, experiencing the same things we are. What does he see? How does he see people? How does he see the cars, the taxis, the traffic, the porters, the confusion, the people coming and going? What does Jesus see?"

"When he saw the crowds, he had compassion on them, because they were harassed and helpless, like sheep without a shepherd" (Matt 9:36).

Opening Your Spiritual Eyes

Learning to see through the eyes of Christ is a process you can begin with this first step. At the dining room table, you and your children can look up the Scriptures that describe Jesus having compassion on the multitudes, the crowds he encountered. (See Matt. 9:36, Mark 6:34, Luke 10:23.) How did he know which ones needed help? How did he help them? What ideas do these passages give you and your family?

After you have studied the Scripture passages, ask God to help you open your spiritual eyes to see as Jesus would see. Before you leave the dining room table, plan a time and place to go see a crowd.

In anticipation of this adventure, pray together. Talk about what to take with you. Be sure the children take their notebooks to write down the needs they see. Young children might like to make some "Jesus glasses" out of pieces of cardboard for this experience. An alternative would be to give everyone an inexpensive pair of sunglasses with the lenses removed.

Where Are the Crowds?

We usually spend our time trying to avoid crowds. Now your job is to find them. Pick a location where a crowd will have a good mix of people, a heterogeneous versus a homogenous group. You want a location where you are free to look at people and study them. You will need to be able to look into people's eyes. See their facial expressions. Determine what their walk and composure tells you about them. Even their shoes can tell you something. Look at what they carry and the way they carry it. Are they vying for attention? Hurried? Bored? Disabled? Do they look at ease, happy, stressed, worried, sad, distracted?

One idea is to go to the mall at a busy time. Or try a high school football or basketball game. Maybe a concert would do. Or the hubbub of a county or state fair. On a busy day the airport terminal would be a good place. You can even try your local discount megastore.

So what would Jesus see if he were with you? Find a place to settle in and watch, to really see the crowd. Hmm. There's a heavy frown on that face. Wonder what his problem is? That one right behind him is talking like crazy to his friend. Must be something interesting in his life.

Here's a person who looks like she just lost her best friend. What a scowl on that face. Wonder what happened? That one on the right seems shy. Whoa, that gal is just plain rude. There's a young mother coming now pushing a baby carriage, carrying another baby, with two little boys following behind. She certainly looks distressed.

Those teenagers over on the right look a bit rebellious by the way they are dressed and acting. They are getting attention. I guess that is what they want. Look at that woman! She walks like she really knows where she is going. People keep bumping into that older couple walking so slowly. What would Jesus think if he were with us right now, looking at this crowd?

That couple looks as if they might be from Mexico. Maybe they are here to find work. Interesting! Hey, there's a Muslim family! You can tell by the women's clothes! Where do they live?

We will never forget September 11, 2001. As we look back at that tragedy, it seems most American Christians had ignored the presence of Muslims in our midst. Now that our eyes are open to seeing them, we realize that people from the Middle East and Asia live all around us. How well do we know them? How well do they know us?

As you look at your world through the eyes of Jesus, you can probably recognize a variety of nationalities by people's physical differences and dress. Our country is a mosaic of peoples with various skin colors, hair colors, and facial features. They have come here as Muslims, Hindus, Buddhists, Shintos, Sikhs, or followers of other religions bringing their religious customs with them. You have taken the first step by seeing them. You are now ready for the next step—friendship.

Your Sphere of Influence

To make friends with people of other nations and cultures, you must first find them in your sphere of influence. But how?

Start with your school district. Have your children tell you about the children of different nationalities at school. Names of children are sometimes a clue to nationality or religion. Find opportunities to invite these children and their parents to your house. You and your children can have the opportunity to make friends with them.

The next time you and your children see people who appear to be from another country or culture in your local grocery or a department store, try starting a conversation. Compliment them on their attire, or say something else that shows you notice their distinctive background. Ask about their country of birth. If you sense you've made a connection, you could invite them to go to the coffee shop in the store. Offer to invite them to your home soon.

One recent cross-cultural friendship opportunity I experienced was on a valet bus from the parking lot at the airport to the terminal. The driver looked as if he were from the Middle East. As I disembarked, I asked, "How long have you been in this country?"

"One year," he replied.

I chatted briefly, thinking I would probably never see him again. Not so. On my return, he was the driver again. This time I started the conversation by asking him if he had many friends in this city. His response brought the opportunity to get his phone number and later invite him to my house.

What Is Compassion?

Jesus saw the crowds and had compassion, pity, sympathy, tenderness, and mercy on them. What did he do? He taught them, fed them, healed them, and met their needs (Matt. 9:35). If he were here beside you today, what would he be thinking? Don't you agree that the Christ of the twenty-first century would still see the crowds and have compassion on them? It seems people are still "like sheep without a shepherd" (Matt. 9:36). That aspect of being human hasn't changed in these last two thousand years.

How do you teach your children to be compassionate? Compassion starts with you. If you don't see the crowds through the eyes of Christ, and if you don't have compassion, your children won't either. Give careful thought to your reactions to the crowds you encounter along with your children. After your children share their thoughts, share yours. Learn to talk about what you see and feel so it is a continual experience.

See and Serve

The Lord will sometimes lay a burden on your heart without the answer as to how to respond. These moments are opportunities. They remind us that his ways are not our ways, and his timing is not our timing. Many years ago I was in Beijing,

China, when the Lord gave me a burden for my guide, who was assigned to me by the Chinese Tourist Agency. I had the privilege of talking to him about God. He knew absolutely nothing about what Christians believe.

I started by talking about God the Creator and all that he had made. Then I shared about mankind sinning and the evil and wrong in the world. Next I told him about a God loving us so much that he sent prophets and more prophets until he finally sent his only son. This Chinese man, Wang, was very interested. He wanted to know more. He asked me, "Does your religion help you with your problems?" A great question—a wonderful opportunity to tell him more about our loving God.

The next morning, Wang took us to Tiananmen Square. People were everywhere. This was in 1981 when people in China hadn't seen many Americans face-to-face. They had never seen anyone with my color of skin, round eyes like mine, and light brown hair. In no time about fifty people had surrounded me just to stare at a strange woman. I couldn't talk with them or they with me, but there the Lord gave me another burden, this one for all the people of China. I saw the multitudes and had compassion on them. Actually, my heart was broken because these people had no way to know about Jesus. I could tell Wang about Jesus because he knew English. But what was I to do about all these others? I didn't speak Chinese, and even if I had, I wouldn't have been allowed to talk to people about Christianity. Not then. Not there.

Three years later, in 1984, the Lord supplied the answer. A Chinese pastor I met told me he wanted to build a church building in China. At that time it was unheard of and impossible. Yet this pastor had a permit from the government and was asking for my help. I didn't have a dime for the funds he needed, but I knew in my heart that this was an answer to the burden the Lord had given me that morning at Tiananmen Square.

I prayed and then got to work doing what I thought Jesus would do. I was able to raise the money, so the church was built. I even went to China for the dedication! The Lord worked it out in his time and his way. He helped me see the people of China through his eyes and showed me how to respond.

Find ways to serve others where your children can be involved. The Yellow Pages is an easy resource for contacting hospitals, nursing homes, social service organizations, and shelters. Your church may have a program to help the homeless, the poor, or a particular ethnic group. Volunteer. In no time, your children will discover new places and ways to help others. Maybe they'll see that the widow down the street needs her lawn mowed or help washing her windows. Maybe they'll notice someone on a street corner that looks homeless. Maybe a neighbor has a new baby and could use a meal. You might simply see someone struggling with too many packages and have your children open the door for them.

In addition to helping those with needs around you, inviting Muslims, Hindus, and Buddhists into your home gives you opportunities to teach your children more about people of other parts of the world. Your children can help you prepare your house for company or cook special foods for your guests. Share with your children your own heart's desire that these new friends will come to know Jesus Christ. Be sure to pray with your children for your new friends.

Children often open the door to reaching others. Their naîveté, innocent questions, or trust in adults may turn conversations in the right direction. When your guest is sitting in your living room, a child might innocently ask, "Do you know about the baby Jesus?" He might say something like, "We're going to church tonight. Do you want to go with us?" A child might even say to your new Hindu friend, "Why do you have that spot on your face?" You can take these questions and use them to talk about Jesus and Christianity. Don't see such questions as embarrassing, but rather as opportunities for your conversation to move in a spiritual direction.

As your friendships develop, you will have opportunities to ask even more questions about your new friends' religions. The apostle Paul gives us an example of this in Acts 17:16–34. These conversations may open a door for you to ask such things as, "How are you assured that you will attain paradise, nirvana, or heaven?" What a privilege it is to share with them the assurance the Lord gives us of being with him in paradise forever.

Mosaic friendships are certainly one opportunity for sowing seed. You may see the harvest, or it may take years before these new friends are ready to accept Jesus Christ as their Savior. Your job, regardless, is to sow. There can be no harvest without the seed being sown. The Lord is the Lord of the harvest.

The Miracle in Mexico

When Kristen was fifteen, she joined the youth group that was going to Mexico for a vacation Bible school in a village near Monterrey. She loves Mexico and goes every chance she can. This time her dad was in charge and he was challenged to take a small group to a new squatters village to reach those children. He chose only veterans of previous teams, including Kristen, because the mission would be more difficult.

The village had no real houses, only lean-tos made out of scraps the people had picked up from dumps. The streets were just dirt paths, and there were barrels to provide water. Upon arrival, they found about thirty kids playing in the dirt, but as they walked the paths and told the kids what they were going to do, the children started following them like the Pied Piper.

Ending up under a tree, the team spent several hours sharing stories of Jesus and his love for children. The next two days were basically the same except every day the group grew larger. Each day they had brought some treats for the kids to finish up the time together. On the third day, Kristen's dad was in front of the kids telling them that they were finished and had some treats for them. All the time he was talking he was distracted by Kristen frantically waving to him from behind the kids.

Kristen brought up the sack of treats and had each kid reach in and get one. They crowded around and each got a treat. That is when Kristen started crying.

"Kristen, what's the matter? Why are you crying?" her dad asked.

"I counted those treats three separate times and there wasn't enough for everyone. I know I counted them right. And three times, too. Dad, it was a miracle. There were not enough treats in the bag for everyone, but everyone got one. God did a miracle."

Kristen and her dad both shed tears of joy and thanksgiving for God producing just in the time of need. It wasn't bread and fishes, and it wasn't five thousand, but it was just enough treats for every child there—a miracle Kristen and her dad will never forget.

An Unexpected Encounter

One summer evening I was taking a walk in my neighborhood. As I had almost reached my turn-around point, I noticed a man walking toward me. He looked like he was from India. As he approached I spoke first. "Excuse me sir, but are you from India?"

"Well, yes, I am. Do you know India?" He responded.

"Oh, I think India is a very interesting country. I have read a great deal about it, and I have some friends there. Do you live around here?" I asked.

"No, no. I live in Calcutta. I am here visiting my daughter and her family. They live in this house," he said as he pointed to the big white two-story house behind him.

I found out that both his daughter and his son-in-law work for a large pharmaceutical company. They have been here for three years. This man and his wife come over every other year for six months. He is retired from a pharmaceutical company in India, and his wife is a retired professor from a university in Calcutta.

I didn't want this conversation to end. Just then a thought came to me.

"Sir," I said, "It would be a pleasure to have you and your family to my house next Sunday evening for tea. Would that be possible?"

"That would be delightful," he replied.

"Oh, I need your phone number and I'll call you," I said. "We can set up the time then. Would that be OK?"

He took a scrap of paper and a pen from his pocket and wrote his name and number. Handing it back to me, he said, "We would be very pleased to come. Just call me. Here is our number."

On Sunday evening this man, Gnanaraj, brought his daughter Issa, son-in-law Sundaram, and grandson to my door. The grandson, Reetom, was carefully carrying a gift for me, a special cake. As I greeted them and invited them in, they took off their shoes and left them at the door, as is their custom in India. Then I brought them into my living room. All of us were excited about getting acquainted and learning about each other. Questions started: Why was I interested in India? Had I known any Indian people before? Was I aware of the Taj Mahal? Would I like to visit India? This was a great time to learn more about their country and what was important to them.

I was prepared with my pictures of India and questions about their country. I also had a map available so they could point out where they lived and other key places of interest. The map was especially helpful in our conversation, giving me a better understanding of that subcontinent of one billion people.

Not long after that evening they called and invited me to their home for dinner. Our relationship is growing. It will take some time to develop friendship and trust, but they are in my prayers. I am their friend, an American Christian friend, and I trust the Lord to use this friendship to bring them to know him as I do.

Your Mosaic Friendships

Before you do anything to make these kinds of cross-cultural connections, what I like to call "mosaic friendships," be sure to pray together as a family, asking the Lord to make available to you the people he wants you to get to know. Your children are a valuable part in developing these friendships. Together, use the eyes of Christ to look for potential new relationships with people around you. Thousands of people, including entire families, have come to the United States. They are everywhere. Just ask God and use the eyes of Christ. He will provide divine appointments for you.

Pray again and again with your children, asking the Lord to use you where he wants. You can show compassion on the multitudes in so many ways. Watch your and your children's sensitivity grow. Go and do whatever the Lord shows you. Experience the joy of service.

A Service of Celebration

You may want to find a container in which to place a record of each of your family's service deeds. A jar or decorated box will do. As each service is completed, write it on a separate piece of paper. At a given time, after your container has several records in it, you can have a ceremony in which you give all your deeds to the Lord. An Old Testament way of bringing an offering to God would be to burn the offering. You could use a campfire circle or a wood-burning fireplace.

Another way to celebrate what the Lord has helped your family do in service to him and to others would be to seal the slips of paper in an envelope and let your children place the envelope in your church's offering plate. (It will be necessary to give the church treasurer or a deacon advance notice of your plan.)

Any way you do it, be sure your children recognize that they have given their time, effort, and compassion to the Lord because he helped them see the world through his eyes. Praise them for learning to see the world through the eyes of Christ, developing his vision for our world.

WHAT YOU CAN DO TODAY AS A FAMILY

1. How would you describe your spiritual eyesight for the world at this time?
2. What is your heart telling you about mosaic friendships?
3. Have your children agree to find five people in the next week that they see have a need. Talk about ways your family can help them.
4. Discuss with your children what you know about Islam, Hinduism, and Buddhism and the need for their followers to know about the true and living God and Jesus Christ. Point out to your children Scriptures that teach about Jesus as the only way to heaven and eternal life.

5. Have your children start a world travel book. Make one section called "Seeing and Serving." Tell them to write down things they see that they think Jesus would see. Later on they can write what they did each time they saw a need and helped meet it. There will also be sections for other experiences named "The World," "Religions," and "Cultures."

A WORLD TRIP—LOCALLY

D ad, look. I have twenty-eight countries on my list. This one, Macau, is a funny-sounding name. Where is it? And here is another one—Sri Lanka. Are these really countries? I never heard of them. What kinds of people live there?"

A "world trip" is an eye-opening experience available now, right in your vicinity. Mark your family's calendar. Sit down with your children and start planning. You will soon discover that much of the world can come to you in your own town or a nearby city.

Pull out those world travel books. Open to "The World" section and have them write down the names of the countries they know something about and can locate on a world map. Wait. That's not enough countries for your family's world trip. You will need to build those lists by exploring your city and seeing how many more countries you can add. Here's how.

Visit Religious Sites

On an actual tour of a foreign country, you nearly always are taken to a monumental cathedral, mosque, historic church, or temple. On this "world trip" you will want to visit religious places as well. Start with your phone book. Turn to the church section of the Yellow Pages. As you carefully look through the listings together, you will find interesting ethnic groups you didn't know were in your vicinity. In some cities you will find Mexican, Korean, Greek, Ethiopian, Bulgarian, Romanian, Eastern, as well as Jewish, Baha'i, Buddhist, Mormon, and Muslim places of worship. Have your children add these places of worship and their addresses to their world travel books. Plan a time to visit each one.

However, more is involved in this part of your world trip than simply visiting buildings of other religions. This is the perfect time to sit down with your kids and talk about the foundations of Christianity. In our American postmodern culture, parents must find opportunities to talk to their kids about their convictions. Christianity is built on faith in one God, his son Jesus Christ, and the Holy Spirit. Jesus' pronouncement that he is *the* way, *the* truth, and *the* life is essential. Other "ways" and other "beliefs" are or will be thrust upon your kids as they grow up.

Your children must know they are to come to Jesus Christ and ask him to be their savior when they feel they are ready to take that step. You want them to know that he is the only Son of God and he is the only truth. Truth is not relative, as so many believe today; it's not simply what you believe but rather what the Bible states. The fact that the only one way to heaven is through Jesus Christ must become a conviction, more than just a belief. What better time to talk about it than when you are getting ready to expose your children to other religions?

You might want to use Josh McDowell's book *Beyond Belief to Convictions* as the basis for your discussion with your kids. You will want to prepare yourself and your family before bringing individuals from other cultures into your life.

What do Hindus believe? With over 330 million gods, they would find it easy to simply add another one. They are not aware that our God is the Creator or that he sent his Son Jesus Christ to show us how to live. They have no concept of a God who loves, cares, and wants to forgive us of our sins. As you get acquainted with them, you will begin to see how you can share the one true living God. There are materials for you to give to them as well. The New Testament is available in most major Indian languages. Many of the Indian people who are in the United States know English as well as you do, so perhaps an English version would be best when the time comes to give them a Bible. There are over four and a half million Hindus living among us.

You will want to research Buddhism with its transmigration of the soul and its attendant, Karma, plus the long agony of searching for inner peace. Originating in eastern and central Asia, Buddhism teaches that suffering is inherent in life and that one can be liberated from it by mental and moral self-purification. Over two and half million people of the Buddhist faith live in our country. More are coming all the time.

What does Islam teach? Muslims and Christians do share a heritage that began with Abraham, but from there the changes are significant. Muslims will challenge you with their concept that we, and people of the Jewish faith, all worship the same God. The Muslim concept of God is that he does change, you earn heaven by your works, and you never know if you will make it to heaven until you are at the door. There is no love in Islam. No forgiveness, no sin, no salvation, no faith, and no relationship with a heavenly Father as we understand these principles. Muslims also believe the Bible is corrupted and the Koran is the only holy book. There are over six million Muslims in the United States.

As you and your kids examine these religions, plus the New Age movement with its seeking for God in several different ways, your children will begin to understand the need for all people everywhere to know the one true God. This is an essential time to discuss the attributes of God, who is loving, unchanging, all knowing, and supreme, and yet who is personal and cares about us as individuals. He cares so much that he adopts us into his family. No other religion can make that claim.

This is the time to remind your children that God sent his Son to give us truth, direction, salvation, and eternal life—a gift for those that believe. Make sure they understand that when we ask God's forgiveness for our sins, he becomes our heavenly Father and loves us with an unspeakable, incomprehensible love.

Your kids should know that there are over sixty prophecies in the Old Testament given four hundred years or more before Christ that spoke of the coming of Jesus Christ. Jesus also gave us his word in many Scriptures, such as:

- "You are right in saying I am a king. In fact, for this reason I was born, and for this I came into the world to testify to the truth" (John 18:37).
- "I am the way and the truth and the life. No one comes to the Father except through me" (John 14:6).
- "You are the Christ, the Son of the living God" (Matt. 16:16).
- When Jesus was asked, "Are you the Christ, the Son of the Blessed One?" he replied, "I am, . . . and you will see the Son of Man sitting at the right hand of the Mighty One and coming on the clouds of heaven" (Mark 14:61–62).

- "Believe the miracles, that you may know and understand that the Father is in me, and I in the Father" (John 10:38).

As you visit various religious buildings and explain other religions, your kids will realize the task of the Great Commission and the need to take the message of Jesus Christ to all nations. You can help your children see the false gods of these other religions, which are, in many ways, similar to the Old Testament false gods of nations other than God's chosen people. The responses people make today parallel the responses of the Israelites who either obeyed God or chose to go their own ways and face the consequences of their disobedience. Talking about them at this age and experiencing other religious practices may eliminate later peer pressure for your children to examine them any further.

Enjoy the Cuisine

Your stomachs can teach you about the world too. What kinds of restaurants do you have in your town? Most of us have eaten Mexican food, but have you tried a Russian or a Greek restaurant? Again your Yellow Pages can be useful. See if you can find German, Indian, Soul, Caribbean, Chinese, Italian, Japanese, French, Irish, Ethiopian, Jamaican, and Russian food choices. What others? Add this information to the world travel books. Set up a schedule for your family to try some of these as part of your "world tour."

Eating foreign food can be an adventure here as well as abroad. I remember well an adventure with food I had in China. My host was the local head of the government of the city of Nanning. With great ceremony he had brought twelve of his colleagues together for a special luncheon. In their culture,

91

where people are seated at the table is very important. Since I was the guest of honor, I was placed at the host's right, facing the door. The other guests were seated according to their position in the government. The usual toasts were given before the meal, but since my host knew that I didn't drink rice wine, guava juice was substituted to accommodate me.

I was really hungry by this time and ready for the food when it finally appeared. As tiny and beautiful China bowls of steaming broth with some unfamiliar pieces of meat were placed before us, I didn't hesitate to get started. It looked and tasted pretty good to me.

"Did you like the soup?" my host asked after I had finished.

"Yes, it was very good," I replied.

"I hoped you would like it. Did you know it was cobra soup?"

I was glad he told me after I ate it rather than before. He went on to tell me why that soup was a special dish and a little bit about how it was made. I discovered anew that you can learn a great deal about a culture by experiencing its foods.

Before you visit the ethnic food restaurants you have selected, be sure your children know something about the common foods of the countries. I'm pretty sure they won't serve you cobra soup, but they will have many other interesting dishes. Many of these restaurants will be happy to give you a recipe of something that you especially like that you could prepare later at home.

Your Tour Begins

You have a list of countries. You have addresses for places of worship. You have restaurants to visit for meals. It's time to load the car with kids, notebooks, lists, and cameras. You are off on your world trip.

The first stop is a department store. Dad needs a hat. You hadn't planned on getting a hat, but shopping, too, is a part of every world tour. In the stores, look at the labels in various clothes items. Going from hats to underwear to nightwear and on to jackets, slacks, shirts, pants, and coats, you will find items made in many different foreign countries. The questions will come.

"Dad, why are all these different countries' names in our American clothes?" "Do the people in these countries make our jeans and jackets and even our underwear for us? Why do they do this?" "Where is Indonesia?" Good questions, which require good answers.

Have your children write down each country name they discovered in their notebooks. They will enjoy trying to pronounce the names of those countries they never heard of and the spellings they have to copy carefully. If that stop was a good learning experience, you may want to take time to check out several more stores before you stop for lunch or a snack at one of your chosen restaurants.

At the restaurant you've chosen for the day, look for owners or employees who come from the restaurant's country of origin. Engage one or two of them in conversation, and see if they will answer questions your family wants to ask about their country. Telling them that you are on a "world trip" can start the conversation. You will find they love to talk about their country if you are interested in listening. So listen and chat. You just might become friends.

The afternoon can be used for tours of some of those churches and temples you located and discussed. If you have called ahead, a representative will be prepared for your arrival and ready to tell you how the various religious practices and beliefs are different from what is known about yours.

Your last stop for the day could be the local police station or the local chamber of commerce, where you can find out where the neighborhoods of the different ethnic groups you have been learning about are located in your city. Sometimes the police station staff can tell you not only where they are located but how large they are and how long they have been there.

Locating More Countries

When you arrive home, the excitement will grow as you look at the long list of countries you have learned about on your tour today. Go to your world map or atlas and have your children look up each country, find the capital, and write it down. Your children can use the encyclopedia or the Internet to research the countries, finding out the population, the people groups, the various religions, the languages, the economy, and the politics. If you use a resource such as *Operation World* (book or software) by Patrick Johnstone, you can even find the prayer needs. Johnstone also has a great laminated map of the world you can order to use on your breakfast room wall. Research on the Internet might answer the questions as to why these people are making our clothes.

Close the first day's trip by praying for each country and some of the people you encountered during the day. Your children will be amazed to see how much of the world has come to them and how much they can learn.

Your family's global viewpoint will continue to change as you put faces and cultural experiences with country names and places. Your global vision will grow as you see the scores of opportunities just waiting for you to explore right in your own backyard. Your hearts will melt as you realize how many of these people have never heard of Jesus Christ. In just one day, your family will have enlarged its global vision and started to see the world as Christ sees it.

WHAT YOU CAN DO TODAY AS A FAMILY

1. Discuss your reaction to people of other nationalities. Have you seen them as hindrances in your community or opportunities?
2. What problems of other cultures bring you the biggest concern these days?
3. Search your local phone book or the largest city near you for places of worship of other religions.
4. Schedule your first world trip. Talk with your children about the different religions you will see, and pray with your kids that as you understand other religions you will find ways to talk to people about Jesus Christ.
5. If God were to speak to you in the area of your greatest culture concern, what do you think he might say?

ON YOUR DOORSTEP

Suppose you woke up this morning in a small apartment in Bangkok, Thailand. It's different than your place at home—quite tiny in comparison, with a small bedroom, a living room, a tiny bathroom, and a bit of a kitchen. Just last night you got off the plane after what seemed like a never-ending flight from Los Angeles. You were lucky enough to find a taxi whose driver could barely understand your English, but he somehow managed to bring you to this place. And now, you are here for a nine-month stay while you study the language.

Exhausted, you fell into bed last night without thinking about what you'd do in the morning. Now awake, you are hungry. Your first activity in this strange city will be to shop for groceries. You're not sure how to do that, but you head for the street below and start walking. Strange place, strange adventure, strange language, strange people, and you're all alone.

Now suppose you have been in Thailand a month and have the grocery and other basics under control. You have found that you can do your class work fairly easily, but you have so much free time left. The evenings and the weekends seem to last forever.

There is only so much TV you can stand or understand. Only so much reading you want to do. You miss your friends and family back home. You are getting homesick. The routine of going to class, eating, sleeping, and getting along each day is becoming monotonous. You pass family groups on the street and in the grocery, friends walking along together, couples having lunch, and you wonder how you can find someone in this big city that you can have as a friend. Lonesome? Yes. Homesick? You bet. Counting the days until you can go home? Of course.

Okay, it isn't your life. You are safe at home with your family and comfortable in your daily routine. But how about those foreign students in your city that have come from a distant culture to earn a degree or learn English? They, not you, experience being thousands of miles from home, being lonesome and homesick. They are searching for a friend in your big city.

Finding International Students

Here is where your entire Great Commission family gets to work. You can be a double winner. You can become those friends that foreign students are seeking. Plus, your children can learn about another culture, how to relate to people of that culture, and more about the world in which your family lives.

Thousands of international students come to this country every year. Having a family like yours as their American friends would enrich their lives. Adventure for your family is waiting out there, and the possibility of introducing international students to the Jesus you serve is limited only by your willingness to reach out to them. It will take a little bit of work, a little bit of your time, and a little bit of your love. However, the effort will produce pleasure, excitement, and productivity that will impact your children and these students forever.

International students are an invisible group, a hidden people right among us at our colleges and universities. Most are young people working on degrees in fields such as medicine, biochemistry, nuclear engineering, neurology, political science, and business. In just a few years these students will return to their homelands—Turkey, China, Iraq, Saudi Arabia. Their homeland may be one where foreign missionaries are not allowed.

Where do you begin to make contact with these students? Start with your local university or college. Find the international student advisor, and tell him or her that you want to develop friendships with some international students and help them with their English. If there is a particular country you are interested in, share that with the advisor.

Next, do some homework. Find out if church or civic groups nearby have programs to reach out to international students. Get in touch with these groups and find out how they work with students. Decide if working through these groups would be a good approach for you.

As a family, read about what you are going to do before you start. A prime source of help in reaching and working with international students is the book by Tom Phillips and Bob Norsworthy, *The World at Your Door*. There are others. Read at least one on the subject.

The next step is to prepare your family. With your globe or world map, locate the country of the student or students you will be meeting. You can talk about that country's culture in your family times. The differences you discover in language, foods, values, religion, and a host of other things can challenge your children. Decide when you will invite an international student to your home and what the occasion will be. Pray as a family about how you want these relationships to develop. This is friendship evangelism. It can be the beginning of a continuing beautiful and hopefully eternal relationship.

Meeting Their Needs

Be ready for some surprises. I remember when we brought two graduate students in nuclear engineering from Taiwan into our home. We drove to the university for the first meeting. Our plan was just to meet them informally and set up a time that we could pick them up and take them to our house for dinner. All went well until we asked if there was anything they needed at that time. There was. They needed us as a guide at the grocery store. They told us that our huge stores were intimidating to them, so full of things they had never seen before. Navigating them through a grocery store would be a great help.

It sounded interesting and easy enough, so we drove them to the grocery store closest to the university. Each aisle became a bigger adventure than the last. They had to stop and examine all the different vegetables and fruits. The bakery was intriguing. The myriads of canned goods called for many explanations. The varieties of frozen items was staggering. The meat counter was unbelievable. The dairy case brought a babble of exclamations. The cards, the toiletries, the drugstore boxes and bottles, the books, and all the other miscellaneous items we daily push our carts past created curiosity and scores of questions from these students.

That experience was interesting for us and educational for them. They had connected with people who could help them understand this new world. We had found two young men from halfway around the world that needed us as friends.

Our next visit with these young men was dinner and an evening in our home. At the appointed time, we drove as a family to pick them up. When we arrived at the university, they were waiting at the curb. Obviously they were excited to be going to an American home. Arriving at our house was like being in that grocery store. It seemed everything needed an explanation. We gave them a guided tour—ordinary enough to us, but very different to them. Our house was not at all like what they had come from in Taiwan.

As we sat down to eat, my husband explained that our family always paused before beginning dinner to thank our Lord for the food he had given us. This thing we call "grace" was new to them, but it was certainly acceptable. The meal and the evening was a great success. They were so pleased to be in an American home and to have American friends.

Over the course of that school year, we brought them to our home several times. The most interesting time was during December. We had prepared a special Christmas dinner for them a week before Christmas. Again they were full of questions. "Christmas in America is so different," they said. "We don't understand what it is all about. Would you tell us?"

This was our first real opportunity to tell them about Jesus. What a privilege to tell the story of God loving the world so much that he sent his Son. They seemed so eager to hear it all. They had many questions, and we welcomed the opportunity to give them answers. Hearing it from the mouths of our sons made it all the more valuable. All the young men knew about Christmas was what was on the TV, in the newspaper ads, and on displays around town and at the university. They thought it a strange mixture of Christianity and commercialism.

Then came the most amusing question of all, at least to our children. "Is Santa Claus Jesus' father?" The moment of laughter was good for all of us. We realized in that instant how very glad we were that we were there for them, to answer their questions and be their friends.

Each time these students came to our home for a visit, they had more questions about our faith: Why is America called a Christian nation when not everyone is a Christian? How is Christianity different from Buddhism? What do we think about Islam? What wonderful opportunities we had to share our faith and influence the minds and hearts of these students. At the same time, we were teaching our children about the world and how to pray for others who do not know Jesus as their Savior.

We had these students to our house numerous times before they returned to Taiwan. Always they were loaded with questions. Before they left we were able to find the address of a Christian church in Taipei and share that with them. We heard from them by mail for several years and then lost touch.

Another occasion with a foreign student haunts me still. I was returning home from India when our plane was delayed in Frankfurt, Germany. As the passengers lined up at the hotel where the airline was putting us up for the night, I engaged in conversation with the young Indian man in front of me. He was on his way to Chicago to assist with some major decision for his company in Mumbai.

"Have you ever been to the United States before?" I asked him.

"Oh yes, I went to a university in Kansas and got my degree," he responded.

After some more conversation I asked him if he had ever been in an American church.

"No," he replied, "I never was asked to go to an American church, and I never got to be in an American home either. I would have liked to be in a home. That is one thing I really wanted to do."

If only someone had taken the time to notice this man when he was a student in the United States, he might have had a completely different experience.

God Provides the Answers

Recently I was enjoying dinner with my newest international student friend, who is from Saudi Arabia. On this occasion he wanted some guidance on how to handle girls. One was calling him a lot, and he didn't appreciate it but was too kind to tell her to stop. As we continued to talk about dating and other situations that had come up at his university recently, our conversation changed to the war with Iraq. Our views weren't quite the same, but that conversation brought the opportunity to talk about God as a God of love. We moved on to talk about sin, forgiveness, holiness, the Ten Commandments, Jesus' two other commandments, truth, and daily living with the presence of God in our lives.

Then he asked me, "What kind of Christian are you? Are you Catholic or what?"

That's an interesting question, coming from a Muslim who is new to the United States and doesn't know anything about Christianity. I had to stop and think (and pray for the Lord to give me his answer).

"Samish," I responded, "Remember your telling me that there are as many different kinds of Muslims as fingers on your hands? Well, there are as many different branches of Christianity as fingers on your hands, too, but we all believe in God the Father, Jesus his Son, and the Holy Spirit. Samish, you have seen churches on many corners in this city. If you look at the names of them, they each have different names. There are Presbyterian, Baptist, Methodist, Lutheran, Church of God, Church of the Nazarene, Wesleyan, and many others.

They are all Christian, but each one is intent on emphasizing different parts of Christianity."

That satisfied him for the moment, so we went on talking about God and his love for us and about God being our Father and we his adopted children. The conversation all seemed to make sense to Samish. I had obviously earned the right to be heard.

Questions like Samish's may surprise you when you bring international students in your home, but they are a welcome surprise. Too often we think everyone understands Christianity as we do. Answering such questions helps us realize how many basic aspects of Christianity are misunderstood by people of other cultures and backgrounds. Afterward you can hold a great family discussion on the questions.

Working toward Results

You can do many things to bring about good results as you connect your family with an international student. Here are just a few:

1. Put up a map in your home of your international student's country. The student can use it to talk about where he or she lives.
2. Have one of your children make a welcome sign in the student's language. If you are unable, have the student help you.
3. Plan for each of your children to do something special for your guest—a song, poem, drawing, or exhibit.
4. Be sure to take pictures of your children and your guest together. Have double prints made so you can give your guest copies and save some for your family's album.

5. Have a photo evening when you show a few family photos and your guest brings some photos from his or her family and country.
6. Arrange picnics, outings, and celebrations that include your international student to help bring everyone closer together.
7. Pray with your children regularly for your new friend.
8. Take the initiative in continuing to contact your student friend after he or she moves away. The student's culture may require waiting for you to be the one to invite rather than the student contacting you.

What impact on your children can you expect as a result of your family building friendships with foreign students? Right before their eyes they can see that not everyone thinks and acts as they do. They can learn that not everyone knows about Jesus. They can develop a heart for the "other" people in our world who don't look like them, act like them, or live like them. They can learn to pray that they may be an influence for the Lord on people who do not have him in their lives.

There it is, right at your doorstep—a Great Commission opportunity for your children, your family, and those foreign students waiting for you to make the first move.

WHAT YOU CAN DO TODAY AS A FAMILY

1. Decide as a family the best ways you can reach out to international students. Agree on a list of desired outcomes.
2. Go to a Christian bookstore or the Web, get a book on reaching international students, and read it with your family.

3. Share the possibilities with your family, and pray together that the Lord will give your family the contacts he desires for you.
4. Call a college or university to start the process of finding an international student.
5. Contact the student and plan your initial meeting.

INVESTING—
NOT THE STOCK MARKET

Take a dollar bill and place it on the table in front of you. Now look at it closely. You've seen lots of these. They go through your fingers like water. If you take this one to your supermarket, just how much can you buy with it? Now think, how valuable would that dollar bill be if it was the last one in your billfold?

Imagine you are in another country. What would be the value of that dollar bill in Afghanistan? What would it be worth if you were a street urchin in India? A runaway teenager in New York?

What is a dollar worth in the eyes of your children? How can you use it to teach your children what's important in life?

Investing in Children

You've heard of international Christian organizations that offer you the chance to sponsor a needy child. Among the many are Compassion International, World Vision, and the India Gospel League.[1] How can such organizations help you invest in your children's understanding of money?

A family in the Chicago area made a decision to sponsor a little girl in India by the name of Ashah Shanti. The sponsoring organization sent a picture of her and a bit of her history and circumstances. That picture took a place of honor on the family's refrigerator door, and the children—Heather, Erin, Bryson, and Allie—learned to pray for Ashah. They put their pennies together with their mom and dad's coins so they could send her gifts for Christmas and her birthday. When letters came from her, they were posted beside her picture on the refrigerator.

Ashah Shanti became important to that family. Because of her, India also became important. When information drifted in from the news media of something happening in India, those children prayed especially for Ashah Shanti, not knowing how she would be affected.

Ashah Shanti had been a street urchin. As a sponsored child, she was taken into the Anderson orphanage in Salem, India, where she learned about Jesus and the love of her "family" in Chicago. She chose to become a Christian. As she grew she learned more about God, the Great Commission, and God's plan for her life. She graduated from high school and chose to become a nurse so she could help the poor in India.

This family in Chicago taught their children to invest in a child in India. In the process, they implanted Christian love and compassion. For thirty-five dollars a month and a commitment to care for someone outside their world, wise parents taught their children that everyone can make a difference in the life of someone else in this world. Best of all, on the other side of the world someone else's life was transformed.

Investing in the Future

You've never heard of Abel Reyna, but he is a successful medical doctor and practicing urologist in Saltillo, Mexico. His is another story of how the Lord uses families to invest in others and change lives.

Abel was a young man from a remote village in the mountains south of Saltillo. He grew up believing in witch doctors and their potions and magic. That was all anyone in his village knew about spiritual things until a missionary came and preached about someone named Jesus. Abel chose to believe in Jesus.

When Abel grew to his teenage years, the missionary took him to Saltillo and enrolled him in the Bible training school. Abel was finishing his schooling when my husband and I and our three sons met him. Getting acquainted, we discovered that Abel wanted to be a doctor. A noble idea, but his family had absolutely no money.

A year later, when we were back in Saltillo, we looked up Abel.

"Abel, how are you doing? How are you coming on your medical future?" We wanted to know, because as a family we had continued to talk about him.

"I will have all my premed courses completed in three months. I don't know yet what I will do then. I have checked with the medical schools in Mexico City, Monterrey, and Guadalajara. The tuition is too high for me. I just don't have the funds. I'm afraid this is the end for now." Abel looked dejected as he shared his fears.

"We'll be praying with you, Abel, to see what the Lord has in store for you," we responded.

Back at home, my husband and I sat down with our three sons to talk about what we could do. At that time we didn't realize the impact this investment opportunity would have on our sons, but we wanted to help Abel. We decided we would supply the tuition if he would handle the rest of his expenses. My husband called Abel in Mexico to tell him what we would do. Elated and empowered, Abel started the long journey to become a doctor.

One Christmas we invited Abel to our home in Kansas. He shared with our boys how Christmas is celebrated in Mexico. It was surprising to him to see how an American family observed the holiday. It was equally intriguing for our boys to understand that there are other ways to celebrate Christmas.

Our family invested in one young man's future, and today he and his family have made a significant difference in the lives of thousands of people in the region of Saltillo. He shares his faith with his patients, and he tells them how God enabled him to be there to serve them. Abel's son is now a doctor as well. Our family ties continue across the border. This God-given relationship, built on a small investment, has lasted many years and impacted the lives of our sons, Abel, his sons, and many others.

Investing in Believing Prayer

A young Cincinnati lawyer named Scott Hicks practices immigration law. He handles cases of people wanting to become U.S. citizens. Scott and his wife, Susan, have two small sons, John and Bryan. They are a praying family, and are teaching their two preschool boys to depend on God. Here is Scott's story.

In January 2001 our church asked for a faith promise for missions. This promise was to be an amount that we would in faith give to God if he would provide it. I really wanted to believe God for an amount that was truly impossible for me. I wanted it to be so big that everyone would know it was God and not me that had provided it. As I prayed and asked God what we should give, I felt drawn to a project that I had just learned about—building a pastor's conference center in India. This project touched something dear to my heart. I have long believed that the way to reach the world is for the church to equip local ministers in each country and then have them win their own people. I had no idea how much money was needed for this conference center, so I asked the associate pastor if he could tell me how much the whole project cost.

A week later he saw me at church and mentioned that the cost was about two hundred thousand dollars. Well, that amount was certainly impossible for me. I had no way of earning that kind of money.

The next Sunday was Faith Promise Sunday. The promise card read, "In faith, I promise to give _____." In the blank I wrote, "the Pastor's Conference Center in Salem."

That night at prayer time I told my boys, five-year-old Bryan and three-year-old John, that we needed to pray that God would provide the money for the project. I explained what it was and how much we needed. Bryan asked how much two hundred thousand dollars was. All I could think to say was that if it were in dollar bills, it would fill his room. That impressed my sons, but it never occurred to them that God might not give it to us for the project.

Every night, without my prompting, the boys prayed for this need. Bryan prayed, "Dear God, please give us the money for the building in India." Johnny echoed, "Thank you, God, for the money for that building in India."

Not three weeks later, I received an unusual call from one of my clients. He told me that he had won the lottery. Much to my shock, my ordinary, hard-working client was now a multimillionaire. A few weeks later, after he had collected the multimillion dollar check, he gave me another call.

"Scott, I need to talk to you. Come over to my office. I am making some decisions," he requested.

I quickly went to his office, where he announced, "Scott, I am thinking of giving thousands of dollars to a number of local churches." This somewhat surprised me because I knew he was Muslim, having been born and raised in the Middle East. As he explained what he wanted to do, I told him that I knew of a church project that could use the money and that I would like to get him some information.

I called my pastor and left him a message. "Pastor, I have a client who might be interested in supporting the project in India. Could you please locate some information and documentation on the project for me to share with my client so he can decide if he is interested?"

My pastor called. "Scott, I have the documentation you asked for, but better than that, the man we work with in India, Samuel Stephens, is in the United States. He will be here next Wednesday. Would your client like to meet him personally?"

My client, Mohammad, agreed to meet him. This was getting exciting. On the day of the meeting, Mohammad arrived early. I told him that this meeting was informational only. I wanted him to understand what the project was and to ask any questions.

When my pastor and Samuel Stephens from India arrived, we all took seats around the conference table. Mohammad pulled out his checkbook. I told him to put it away, that we just wanted to give him the information about the project. Mohammad kept it out. At this point he pushed his checkbook toward me and said, "Write the check."

"Sir," I replied, "this is only an informational meeting. First, listen to these men. They are prepared to tell you all about this project."

"Scott, write the check," he insisted.

Again I told him, "Mohammad, as your lawyer, I advise you to listen and not give yet."

His response was to tear a check out and hand it to me as he said quite emphatically, "Scott, write the check!"

Having had some experience with arguing with him, I knew I was not going to get anywhere. I asked, "How much?"

"One hundred thousand dollars," he replied.

I wrote the check for a hundred thousand dollars to the India Gospel League and pushed it over for his signature. He signed it and handed it to Samuel. Samuel and my pastor were more or less in shock and could hardly speak, having never before witnessed anybody arguing to give so much money to a ministry. My pastor recovered and asked if we could pray for Mohammed. At this point he said, "No. I need to leave." We watched in awe as he got up and walked out.

At home that night I told the boys that God had answered part of our prayers. Their reaction was, "How much?" and then, "Oh, okay." Then we started praying for the rest of the money. (The project turned out to need $250,000.)

Every night the boys prayed without any reminder. "Dear God, please give us the rest of the money for that building in India." In December we got word that a pastor of another church had called and inquired about the project. When told that $150,000 was lacking, the pastor said that his church would fund that. Within a year the entire funding was provided.

That night I told Bryan and Johnny that God had completely answered our prayers that all the money had been provided. Again their reaction was nonchalant. "Okay. Thank you, God, for giving the money for that building in India." Of course God provided. What else was he going to do?

When construction neared completion, I was invited to attend the dedication ceremony. I asked the boys if we could pray that God would provide the money for my airline ticket to India and also the money I would lose by not working during the time of the trip.

A week or so later, I was talking to a client from India. He is a devoted Muslim and very active at the local mosque. I mentioned to him that I might be going to India for a celebration. He asked where and why. I told him the whole story. He immediately said, "You must go. That is your responsibility!"

"Of course I would like to, and I am praying for the money for a plane ticket and my expenses while I am gone," I responded.

"Well, I will get you the ticket," he said. "This is God's work, and you must be there."

That evening I told Bryan and Johnny what he had said. Again their reaction was, "Well, of course." Now they are praying, "Dear God, please give Daddy the rest of the money to go to India." I can only expect that God will do so.

113

In the boys' bedroom we have a big world map. Bryan and Johnny both know exactly where India is. Using the map, we have begun praying for other countries. We have a book with information on each country and prayer concerns for each one. Most nights, we unroll the world map and see where that night's country is. We talk about the concerns for that country, and then we each take one concern and pray. Their prayers are simple ones such as "Dear God, please let them finish showing that movie," (the JESUS film) or "Dear God, please help the churches get along better," or "Dear God, please let people tell about you so they can tell other people about you."

Investing in Our Children

Children learn early in life that money is important. From their parents they develop the concepts of how to use it. As they are included in your family decisions in giving to missions, children realize how important money is to you and how you use it for God's kingdom. They learn from your obedience to Jesus about reaching the world. As they see you investing in missions and helping to expand the kingdom of God, they grow up walking in your footsteps claiming their own values and investments. What better footsteps for them to walk in than yours!

WHAT YOU CAN DO TODAY AS A FAMILY

1. Talk with your family about how you view money as a resource for investing in missions.
2. Discuss a family financial commitment to missions.
3. Recall times when God supplied funds for something after you prayed. Celebrate one of these events.

4. Begin your search to find a missions project that speaks to your heart, and explain it to your family. Bring your children into decisions about investing in the project.

5. Include your missions project in your daily prayers with your children.

13

GIVE IT A TRY—
SHORT-TERM MISSIONS

Which do you like best, challenges or fun? You can have both and an adventure with the Lord and for the Lord on a short-term missions trip.

A short-term missions trip to Mexico totally changed my life and the direction my husband and I were heading. Our trip was when our boys were in grade school. At the time, we didn't know anything about missions. Sure, we knew about the Great Commission, but what did that have to do with us? Wasn't that Jesus' instruction to his disciples? That was our thinking until a friend challenged us to go to Mexico and see what was going on there.

Accepting challenges was part of our life. We had already accepted several—building our first home (we built it ourselves), moving halfway across the country, starting a new church. Here was a new challenge and we were ready to accept it. After Christmas that year, we loaded up the boys and headed for

Mexico. We didn't know any Spanish; in fact, we knew nothing about Mexico. But our adrenaline rose as we drove our car south and across the Rio Grande.

Finding the mission station was no problem, and we received a tremendous welcome. The people seemed so glad to have us. We spoke the few Spanish words we were able to pick up along the way, tasted all kinds of Mexican food, tried to drive like the locals, and bought gasoline in liters instead of gallons. We experienced so many new ways of doing things. Most significantly, our eyes were opened to the full meaning of God's church. The church is the body of believers in whatever country, whatever circumstances—Christians who know the Lord and worship him in spirit and deed. It was a glorious experience to worship with Mexican Christians.

That trip changed our understanding of the Great Commission and missions. We had learned in school that Europeans discovered the United States and Latin America. They came to the United States because of *God*. In contrast, Latin America was discovered because of the search for *gold*. The difference is in the *G*'s. The driving force for these explorations made all the difference in the world. On this trip we had seen and experienced the difference in the *G*'s.

Because of this trip, missions took on a different meaning. We saw, we made new friends, we got a new vision, and we knew we were to use that experience as the Lord directed us. It was evident that the people of Mexico could use our help to get the gospel of Jesus Christ to their world. We felt commissioned to help them learn about Jesus and tell others.

Missions trips take you to totally new worlds—new environments, different languages, new reliance on God, and new understandings of the Great Commission. If they can do all of these things for you, what can they do for your kids?

What

A short-term missions trip is a planned excursion of a group of Christians to another location, country, or culture to offer practical help to the local people to accomplish one or more of their programs or goals. "Short-term" usually means one to three weeks, but a trip also could last a month or two.

The most well-known type of short-term missions trip takes a team of workers to construct or renovate a church, a school, a clinic, or some other building. These trips are often referred to as work camps. All who go on these trips are expected to work hard. When your children are old enough to do physical labor, consider taking them with you on a work camp. You will return with an important experience and family memory of having made the world a better place in one small location through the physical work of your hands.

Another common short-term missions trip is one that takes people who can provide a special program such as vacation Bible school or a musical presentation. These trips are typically organized by church or school groups as outreach and learning experiences for teens. If you have a child who has musical or other kinds of presentation skills, you can begin at an early age talking to that child about ways to use that gift for others, especially those of other cultures. Watch for opportunities for your children to minister through their specific gifts.

Other common trips provide specialized services, for example, a group of doctors, or a team of pastors share their expertise. Sometimes these trips will take a youth or two to help. If a child of yours would someday like to become a doctor, dentist, or pastor, you can look for trips that would provide such opportunities.

Still another type of trip is to help local people after a disaster such as an earthquake, major storm, or flood. These trips are similar to work camps, but can include a wider variety of people—men, women, and children—who go to help however needed. Media coverage of children living in garbage dumps in Haiti and families living in tents because their homes were destroyed by an earthquake in Guatemala is more than mere news—it is opportunity knocking on your door. Your kids see these reports, too, and when they realize they can use their muscles and energy to help those people in the midst of their disaster, they are ready to pack their bags. If you go on one of these trips as an entire family, there is almost no age limit for taking children along, since they will be in your direct care.

One other type of trip, sometimes called an eyewitness trip, offers participants an overview of a ministry. It takes place in a particular area for the purpose of building greater understanding of missions work in general. It may include several countries' needs and ministries. These trips are often precursors to other trips by participants, who go home with new understandings about the Great Commission. Their hearts are stirred, making them want to get involved in additional missions work.

Regardless of the type of trip or its stated primary purpose, the ultimate purpose of all short-term missions trips is to express God's love to those in need. These experiences are not only times to work *for* the local people but to work *with* them, and to share the love of Christ and his message. Trip members go to give, and they do, but most often they receive as much or more than they give. That seems to be God's way of rewarding those who go.

Where

Most often, short-term missions trips are to locations in the Western Hemisphere that are relatively accessible. Mexico, for example, is a great place to have a work camp. Haiti is the poorest country in our hemisphere, making it a strategic place to go for evangelism, medical help, and relief efforts. Nicaragua is a Central American nation particularly open to church teams. Other Latin American countries such as Honduras, Panama, Guatemala, the Dominican Republic, and islands in the Caribbean are readily accessible and welcome teams from the States.

Teams are welcomed further away too. Romania, Bulgaria, Eastern Europe, and Africa are great places to serve. You can almost literally pick any country because there are always needs, the world has troubles, and Christians are called to help. The proximity of countries in the Western Hemisphere often reduces the cost of both time and money. Those considerations, however, should not stop you from going to help those further away; especially when the effort to spread the gospel in that location might be of greater long-range benefit than other more commonly visited locations.

Why

Raising Great Commission kids means your children must see firsthand what it is like to be involved in some process of changing a part of the world for Christ. I have witnessed the transforming effects of missions trips on more than seven thousand people over the past forty years. I don't think you or your kids can fully understand the Great Commission without having a missions experience. These experiences will teach you and change you.

Have you ever heard kids say they need a new CD or a video game? When they see the life situations of people in another country, they are struck by the poverty and hunger.

When your kids realize how people they now know personally live without so many things we consider basic, it changes their definition of *need.*

I was in a tiny, remote village in Mexico. Not the kind you see in the airlines brochures. Not the kind you see when you drive across the border to do some shopping. Just a dusty, quiet village where people quietly work at the common task of starving.

I was with a team that was checking on a ministry to children in this village. Word had gotten around that visitors were coming, and they were frantically preparing so everything would be just right for the guests. Nothing would do but to have a special program with the boys and girls performing for the guests.

It was a cold day. The fire in the crowded building filled the air with smoke, but it provided some warmth for the families who packed in to see the program. Near me was a mother with a baby. I noticed how thin and sad the child's face was as she let out a sad, mournful scream. The mother rocked the child, petted her, and cooed a Spanish lullaby, but nothing would quiet the baby. With an apologetic smile, the woman turned to me and spoke in broken English, "Please excuse my baby. She has not eaten for a long time. She hasn't gotten used to being hungry yet."

I couldn't speak. Her words broke my heart. I was looking through the eyes of Christ seeing pain and suffering. This experience redefined the word *need* in my heart and soul from that day forward.

An experience similar to this one happens on almost every trip in almost every country to missions team members. That's why you and your Great Commission kids must go and see for yourselves.

Who

You are never too old to go on a short-term missions trip if you are physically able, but you can be too young. Except for special family missions trips, in my opinion, a child who wants to go on a short-term missions trip should be at least twelve and preferably fifteen or older to get the best benefit of these trips. Why? Small children need adult care. They rarely are an asset to a team. On a trip, team members need to be able to evaluate the situations they encounter, respond appropriately, accept responsibility for their actions, and follow the Lord's direction. Returning home, they should "be" different and they should "do" differently because they have seen the struggles in other parts of the world.

As parents, you will benefit greatly from a short-term experience yourself. Start with a work camp or an eyewitness trip. If you have professional services to offer, consider a trip with your peers. If it is good for your kids, it is good for you too.

How

Churches, organizations, and humanitarian groups plan and take Christians on short-term missions trips. Check first with your pastor about a trip. What trips has your church sponsored in the past? What is planned for the future? Check also with other churches or parachurch organizations in your area.

Before you or your kids sign up, check out the track record of the sponsor. References will give you the assurance you need. Do they take adequate care of the team members with respect to their travel, accommodations, health, and dietary needs? Check with some people who have traveled with them before. Is the spirit of the group one that promotes the cause of Christ?

Another necessary caution these days, because of the rapid growth of short-term missions, is to be 100 percent sure that the trip will be of benefit to the national church in that location. I have heard of a church in Mexico that is painted every year by ambitious North American church groups. If that church doesn't need a new coat of paint every year, then that kind of trip only serves the need of the painters. As you check out the sponsor, also carefully check out the trip project. Short-term mission trips must be of mutual benefit and not just a travel opportunity for people looking for an adventure or a "fun trip" to a new place.

After you are comfortable with the credentials of the sponsoring organization, meet with the team leader. An experienced leader is a must. Your trip will require careful planning, adequate pretrip training sessions, and an assurance that all health needs will be met. The leader's concept of why he or she and the team are going and how they will relate to the local people is an important pretrip conversation point. Team members must know they are going to serve. They will want to relate to and learn from the national people and be a Christlike example all the time.

The Joy of Learning

After you are committed, the names, locations, and other details of your destination take on new interest. Where is Haiti or Honduras or your specific destination? What is the common language? How far is this place from home? How will you get there? What are the people like? What are the religions? What is animism? What is syncretism? If the Catholic church has a presence there, how is it different from the Catholic church in the United States?

Be sure to share all the details of travel preparation with your kids. They need to know why they must have passports and immunizations. They will begin to realize that where they are going is a foreign world, and everything will be different from home.

Keeping a daily journal is important. Journaling should begin well before the departure date. Starting early gets trip members in the habit of journaling before they go. Challenge them to record their thoughts, expectations, and even fears as the departure approaches. Together you could come up with a list of questions that your kids could respond to in the journal.

Fantastic as it may be, the trip will not remain alive in your memories forever. No one can remember the details, impressions, and feelings if they aren't written down. This journaling experience is a journey with the Lord, and your kids need to record every day as it unfolds. What if Moses hadn't kept a record of his experiences? What if Luke failed to record what happened on those trips in Acts?

Journaling should continue when your kids return home. They can look over their experiences and analyze their importance as they write down what they learned. With your guidance, your kids can see how they are growing spiritually. Journaling also can help them decide how they are going to be different every day once they've returned home.

Every missions trip is different. Every team is different. Every purpose is different. Your kids will learn to do things they never dreamed. Besides carrying cement, painting a church, or constructing a house, they will learn to take care of themselves. Have they had to wash that many dishes before? Can they help cook for that many people? What about cold showers or washing clothes in the creek? Or waiting until everyone else has something to eat before they do?

They learn to see needs and meet them; to use their eyes and hearts and ideas from the Lord as they pray to solve the problems; to forget what they want and be content with what they get. They learn that two can do more than one (Eccles. 4:9); that diversity need not be a deterrent; that giving joy brings joy to oneself (Prov. 11:25); that a friend loves at all times and a brother is born for adversity (Prov. 17:17); that competition and individualism may not be honored in all cultures; that the Lord is in other countries just as he is in the United States.

The Joy of Giving

Going on a short-term missions trip takes money. Raising funds for a trip brings wonderful lessons about giving. Regardless of the type of trip or the cost, your kids should be involved directly in raising funds for the trip.

Make your fund-raising a family project. List everyone you can think of that might be willing to help financially. Grandmas and grandpas are usually willing. So are aunts and uncles, Sunday school teachers, and close friends. Help your kids write letters asking for prayer and financial help. Then share how much money is needed and ask people to help sponsor your trip. The letters should let sponsors know that their prayers are particularly needed during the trip and that they will receive a special report when the trip is completed. Some people are inundated with appeals, so consider carefully whom you ask.

One of the many things about giving that you and your children will learn is the generous, unselfish spirit of people everywhere. In the beginning of our family's experiences in missions, I thought we Americans were the ones doing all the giving. It cost us money, time, and effort to go on these trips. While we were on mission, we worked and helped the locals build churches, clinics, or schools. We provided funds for our own food. Our work and our time was our gift to these people, our fellow Christians. All of that was the joy of giving, we thought. We had lots to learn.

Our organization, Project Partner with Christ, had been asked to build a church in the mountains of Guatemala not too far from the capital city. It was relatively easy to find willing workers for that trip. While we were there, we poured ourselves into the task. A church building, ready to hold services, was constructed in just twelve days as we worked side by side with the local Christians. We felt good about what we had given to these people.

On the last day of the work camp, we were invited to a neighboring village church to hold our last service together. The local people worked especially hard to make this final gathering a memorable time for us. Fresh-cut boughs from sweet-smelling pine trees covered the floor. The tantalizing smell of hot and sweet tamales wafted through the evening air. This was a real celebration, a Guatemalan treat just for us. Our team had finished constructing a church, and these village people in these high mountains had prepared this good-bye party for us.

Those tamales were so tasty. After we finished them, we gathered in the church. Our group sat among the congregation on long wooden benches. The women sat on one side, the men on the other. No one seemed to be bothered that there were no backs to the benches. My husband, Chuck, was on the platform with the pastor and some elders. The church was overflowing. Heads were poking in the windows. When the service began, we joined our voices in singing with them. We had learned how to sing along even if we didn't know the Spanish words.

As the service progressed, I heard the pastor say in Spanish that they were going to take an offering. Our team didn't know Spanish, so they didn't understand what he had said. Of course an offering is expected in a church service, but as he continued talking, I heard him say that this offering was for us, the visitors from the States. *What?* I thought. *Why would he do that? We are the ones that have money. These people are poor. The average wage around here is only eighty cents a day. They can't do this.*

The ushers came around with a bag on a long pole. (That was their offering plate.) They skillfully extended that pole in front of their own people, ignoring our group. None of our people seemed to understand what was going on. Then the ushers took their poles to the front and dumped the money into a tray on the altar. The pastor stepped down and counted the offering. At the end of the song, he called my husband over and presented this special gift to him.

"This gift is in appreciation for all of you coming down here and helping our people," the pastor said proudly. "We want to give you this offering for you to use for gasoline for your airplane. We know it costs lots of money, and we want to help too. Your being here means a lot to all of us."

Tears started running down Chuck's face. He was overwhelmed. He stumbled over his words as he tried to thank these people. We had given our money in many offerings on our trips, but never had anyone taken an offering for us. What precious people. We would never forget them, our brothers and sisters in the Lord. What an expression of love.

How much was that offering? It amounted to $5.60. Not much in our economy, but it represented one person's average daily wage (eighty cents) for seven days of work. Seven is the perfect number in the Bible. A perfect gift.

That amount wouldn't make much difference in filling the huge fuel tank on our airplane, but it made a tremendous difference in our spirits and our hearts. As we took off the next morning, our plane's wings lifted us up over the mountains where these people lived. Our spirits lifted in praise to God as well. These people had expressed the joy of giving. God had knit our hearts together. We were seeing God's world through new eyes—through God's eyes and with his heart and understanding.

The Joy of Serving

The joy of serving others, of making a difference in a foreign country, is a wonderful, fulfilling experience. Maybe the joy is in putting on a roof, painting a church, building a simple home, providing a vacation Bible school, or responding to a sudden disaster. But there's more.

The joy of serving also is experienced on a missions trip as team members realize the agenda is not theirs but is instead what the people they have come to serve want and need. I remember a time when we were helping build a church. We felt the wall should be at a certain place because that is the way we would do it at home. It would be too close to the next building. The pastor didn't want it that way. We had to remember we were there to serve, not just to build a church. It needed to be done their way.

As your kids learn to serve, they will also learn to do it the way the host wants it done, which may not be the way it is done at home. This, too, is a great learning experience, as so often in our American culture we believe we have all the answers.

When we go to serve, we have no idea of the full impact of our giving. In 1972 Nicaragua experienced a devastating earthquake. Tall buildings collapsed, homes were devastated, and thousands of people had no shelter, no food, no water—nothing. My husband and I sent out word that we were scheduling teams and flying them down to help for two weeks at a time.

Christians care. We had hundreds of volunteers. We filled our forty-passenger airplane time and again with people who wanted to serve. They took tents, medical supplies, water, and clothing with them for distribution. They pulled away rubble and built shelters. They fed the hungry, bound up the wounded, and joined their voices in praising God in church services even though those services were often held under a tree.

The work of these teams made a great impact on the government. General Zamoza was president at that time. Amazingly he called my husband, Chuck, to his office, telling him that he had planned for the following year to be called the Year of Reconstruction. However, because we had come and brought people who really cared and helped, he was naming it instead the Year of Reconstruction *and Hope*. Our teams made a significant difference.

The Joy of Being a Parent

Sending your kids on a missions trip takes prayer and the ability to let go. It also provides a special blessing as you express in a new way to your kids that you are behind them in their obedience to the Lord. Here are some excerpts from a letter a father wrote to his daughter on her first mission trip. The names are what the dad and daughter tease each other with at home.

Hello SingSing,

Welcome to one of your most exciting missions yet! Remember, you are part of a family with this purpose: Our mission is to glorify God by creating a safe and fun place where we can help each other to discover and develop our full God-given potential for the purpose of sharing Christ's love with others and strengthening the local church.

Even though you will be far away from us for a few days, we're still a team and our family will be accomplishing its mission through you. We know that God will be with you. While you're there, please do the following:

1. Read Psalm 118 every morning and Psalm 91 at night, and remember that every day is a gift from God in the morning and that his steadfast love endures forever. Remember that God is your fortress every night and that under his wings you will always find refuge. Take time to pray each day.

2. Be a helper—look for ways to share Christ's love. Be a blessing to the people you are with. (You're very good at this!)

3. Have fun. Don't be afraid to try something new. Be yourself. You are a wonderful person to have fun with.

4. Take good notes. Write in your journal and take pictures so that you can report on your mission when you get back.

I love you more than all the taco stands in Mexico! Have a wonderful trip—I will be praying for you.

I'm very proud to be your dad.

StinkBomb over and out

The Joy of Connecting

Your kids will discover the oneness of God's family. They will learn we are all in this world together. They will sing the chorus "We are one in the spirit, we are one in the Lord" with new insight. It will flood their hearts as they carry bricks or cart cement, mix paint or sweep up dirt. We are one.

They will learn to depend on God, to be connected to him. They will learn to "hang loose." Things often don't go as planned. They will have to work around problems they never knew existed. Things don't work the way they should. There may be too much free time or no free time. The meals may be great, or they may have the same food again and again. The material may not arrive, or they might not have material.

The project may finish too early, or the project might not be completed before it is time to leave. So whom do they learn to depend on? They learn to ask their heavenly Father to work matters out according to his plan and purposes.

What Do They Appreciate?

When your kids return from a missions trip, they will have a different view of so many things. The good old U.S.A. takes on a new character. Their family and heritage have gained importance. They hadn't realized before what tremendous support and love they have from Mom and Dad. Their room, their own bed, their own shower are now luxurious. Ah, such comfort. Their culture is great to fall back into. Their food—bring on the hamburgers and the pizza. Their church. The Christian community. A greater appreciation for all of life around them, including their family. Now they see things differently.

You will all discover the trip was more than worth the time, the effort, and the money. The trip experiences will be with your kids throughout their lives and impact many decisions they will make about their future. Their eyes have seen, their hearts have melted. Life takes on a different view. Your kids will have learned to accept the Great Commission as their own.

WHAT YOU CAN DO AS A FAMILY

1. Pray that the Lord will give you direction and guidance in finding a short-term missions experience that's right for your family.
2. Meet together as a family and discuss the concept, the possibilities, and the process of going on one of these trips.

3. Assign family members the task of locating possible opportunities coming soon.
4. Work out a plan to raise the funds. Set a goal and a date for completion.
5. Have a family commissioning service the night before departure.
6. Upon return, line up opportunities to speak to those who helped finance the trip, to classmates, and to others who would be interested in hearing about these experiences. Don't leave it to chance.

14

A FAMILY ADVENTURE

You've got to be kidding! Why would an entire average, middle-class family that has so much going for them drop everything and take their children to spend a year on the mission field? Is that really what the Lord wants for them?

They have a really nice house in a beautiful neighborhood. Their kids, at eight, ten, and twelve years old, are in a good school district. Their church is great, plus it has a great missions program. They're not too far from the kids' grandparents. The culture around them is just like them—comfortable. Then why would they consider such a radical change?

Think about this scenario. What if it were you who sold your house, negotiated an extended leave of absence from your job, stored your furniture, loaded up your kids, and headed off to another country for a year?

Yes, that's what I said. Maybe it's a year in Austria at a Muslim refugee camp. Or a year in the interior of China. Would you have to be crazy to do it? Some people would think so. What do you think? What would it do for your kids, and for you?

I've checked with some families that have done or are in the middle of doing this very thing. They give positive, glowing reports. Are they crazy? They don't think so. I don't think so. They talk about the impact on the nationals, their kids, themselves, that part of the world, and their church at home.

I asked these families why, with so much going for them, they'd drop everything and take their children to spend a year on the mission field. The parents told me they wanted their kids (and themselves) to know how to live in another culture. They knew that sooner or later their kids would question the values of their own culture. Living overseas for a year or even two would offer a different perspective for them on materialism, isolationism, justice issues, busyness, rights, fairness, learning to be the minority, relationships, soccer games, and so on. Besides, they said, they want to serve the Lord as a family.

Maybe it's not for every family, but some are greatly blessed by moving in this direction. Let me tell you about two families who made this choice.

Jim and Cindy's Family

Jim and Cindy both had a taste of missions experience in college. A missions major at Moody Bible Institute, Cindy was involved in Campus Crusade. During his last year of medical school, Jim took a three-month short-term mission trip. Together they joined a church where missions was important. They wanted to pursue missions as a possible long-term career, so they took a trip to Kenya. God did not seem to open this door but they determined to return someday. Their life continued going well. Along came three youngsters. They were the great American family—he was a doctor, she a stay-at-home mom. Fifteen years later, they reevaluated their life and future. Were they spending their lives the way God wanted them to? If not, what did the Lord want them to do?

Jim and Cindy again felt God calling them to the mission field, but in a different way than most people think of missions. They wanted to serve together as a family long enough to really have a full experience. Yes, a family with an eleven-year-old, a nine-year-old, and a six-year-old. So what would this calling mean? They would leave behind their suburban lifestyle, their super-nice house, the great area where they lived, and the kids' schools. They would move to a new country, Kenya, to a mission station with a hospital where they heard there was a huge need for another doctor, and to an American school where the kids would get a great education.

Jim and Cindy sold their house. They had decided they wanted to downsize and simplify their lifestyle. They gave away, sold, and stored their furniture. They made the necessary financial and housing arrangements, packed their bags, and went off to Africa for a year.

How did they manage it? They used the equity from their house to live on during that year in Africa. They enrolled their children in the missionary kids' school located next to the hospital where Jim worked. Cindy worked as a volunteer in the hospital and helped teach a Bible class to nursing students. Together they taught a class at the local Bible college. As a family, they were involved in many school activities and ministries with their new Kenyan friends.

At the end of their one-year commitment, the family returned to the States. They found a home close to the one they once had. The kids went back to the schools they'd left a year ago. And Jim was given back his position in the medical partnership he'd left to go to Africa.

Jim and Cindy learned a lot, but their kids learned even more. They rubbed shoulders with missionaries from all over the world and nationals from Kenya of every economic class. They used their experience and gifts to serve the needs they saw around them. They learned to love God's world in a way that marked their lives significantly. They came to appreciate the diverse world of the mission field.

The kids had a new desire to get to know students of color and other ethnicities. They had more compassion for those who were less privileged than they. Their changed worldview was evident through their choices of activities and church commitments in the following years.

To this day the family talks often about the significance of that year in Africa. Before Africa they were overextended with activities and commitments. After Africa, they were more cautious with commitments, and the family operated differently because of the unique bond of shared experience.

The long-term benefits to the family? The oldest child returned to Kenya after college to serve as a dorm mom at the school for missionary kids where she attended that one year. Her fiancé served at the school for four months as a volunteer. They are now married and he is going to seminary. She is presently working for a Chinese children's adoption agency. She and her husband talk of returning to Africa. The second child has tutored Sudanese immigrant children and studied teaching English as a second language in college. Recently married, her husband is going to seminary also. The youngest is in college majoring in Christian ministries and heading on a short-term mission trip this summer. Jim is now traveling extensively with Campus Crusade for Christ's AIDS education program. Cindy writes curriculum for short-term team members and has trained team leaders for the short-term missions program in their home church.

A great return on a year's investment.

Dave and Claire's Family

Dave and Claire and their two girls chose China for their family missions experience. Having been on short-term mission trips before they were married, Dave and Claire had made a commitment to each other that they would do something in the future to help meet the deep needs they saw in other countries. When they sensed the Lord telling them it was time, Dave went to his employer of seventeen years to ask for a leave of absence. He was told it wasn't an option. If he wanted to go, he would forfeit his job. The family went anyway.

Dave arranged to teach business courses at the university through Educational Services Exchange China. Claire was kept busy with basic living tasks in Bengbu and volunteer work at a children's home. Their children were only two and four, so school was not an issue.

Their life in China was not without difficulties. Instead of piling into a car, family members had to walk everywhere until they mastered the bus system. Laundry had to be done every other day for lack of adequate clothing. Instead of popping into an American-style supermarket whenever they had food needs or wants, they had to go to the market first thing in the morning, just after the animals were slaughtered and the meat set out in the open air. At first it seemed odd to see open windows on a cold winter day when there was ice and snow, but they soon learned most people did not have heat. At times they didn't either.

Their primary missions goal was to meet Chinese college students, teach them conversational English, and plant seeds to bring Christ into their lives. The missions agency they were working with had already proven that Christian teachers were making a measurable impact on China. Within a few months after they settled in, Chinese students were coming to their apartment. A small group Bible study formed.

The year turned out to be most profitable in another way. They learned to place a greater value on family time. They began praying together regularly, and that practice has stayed with them. When they returned, they began investing time in international students in their city. "It was a most profitable year for us, and we plan to go back someday," said Claire. "It was a tremendous experience for all of us to serve the Lord in that way. And, to our surprise and joy, Dave ended up landing an even better job at the company that wouldn't give him a leave."

Your Family's Story

You've heard the story of these families. Maybe what they've done is for you. Maybe it isn't. Ask the Lord. He'll let you know. Then follow his direction. Your children are with you a few short years, and you only live this life once. Here are two resources if you are interested in learning more about family mission adventures: *Essential Guide to the Short Term Mission Trip* by David Forward and *Mack and Leeann's Guide to Short-Term Missions* by Mack and Leeann Stiles.

WHAT YOU CAN DO TODAY AS A FAMILY

1. Discuss these families' adventures. Determine if a family missions experience is something you want to investigate.
2. Write down in two columns all the advantages you can think of and all the disadvantages of a long-term missions experience. Discuss them.
3. Pray together for the Lord's direction. Take a week for individual prayer, then come back together to share what you believe the Lord wants you to do.

THE ROLE
OF THE EXTENDED FAMILY

Ask any grandparent about his or her grandchildren, then step back as the pictures fly. I thought my first grandchild was perfect, but now with nine of them—I can really brag.

They were so tiny and precious when they first came into this world. I remember looking at those innocent little faces and wondering what their lives would hold. I watched each one grow, learn to walk, stumble, and determine to get up and go again . . . a preview of life here on earth.

There are times I'm not Donna, Mrs. Thomas, or Paul's mom. I am six-year-old Johnny's grandma. I haven't had a course in grandmothering. How do I know what I am supposed to do? I know I am supposed to love him. That is easy. I've heard that grandmas make cookies. I can do that. I understand grandparents like to give things to their grandchildren. No problem.

I'm still working on this grandmothering thing. New ideas come all the time.

For example, what gifts do grandparents give? I must stop first and think about the grandparent I want to be. If I have twenty or so years left to influence my grandchildren, what impact do I want to make? A legacy—totally different from figuring out if I can leave them an inheritance in my will. That's just money. Totally different from giving them things to play with or wear or use and then discard. Those are just things. I want to leave them a part of me, a part of what I think is important, a part of what has been my purpose in life. I had better think about my legacy to them and plan it well.

Building a Legacy

Step number one is to talk with my three sons and their wives about my understanding of grandparenting and the leaving of a legacy. We must be on the same page. I want to help them with their task of raising Great Commission kids, but I don't want to get in their way. It's a team effort. They are the coaches, the ones to call the plays. I am simply one player in their children's lives.

After talking these ideas over and listening to their suggestions, I knew what to do. Yes, I could be a grandmother they will be proud of. I could be involved in specific ways in my grandchildren's growing-up years to develop the legacy I want to give them.

The Basket

One idea that came to me was making their trips to Grandma's house exciting by reworking my picnic basket. Here, I thought, was a great opportunity to plant some seeds of the gospel in those little minds. I'd send a letter to each grandchild who was old enough to understand. I'd tell each one I had a special basket at my house, filled with presents, all wrapped up and waiting for them to come. In each letter I'd put a list of Bible verses tailor-made for that child to memorize. They would know that whenever they came to see me, the basket would be waiting for them. They could have any present they wanted from that basket if they could quote one of their Bible verses and the Scripture reference.

Before long, two of them came to my home. Allie and Nicole tumbled out of the car and ran to me. They were jumping up and down and reciting their Scripture verses. This was better than I'd ever dreamed.

Slowing them down, I took Allie first to the basket. Her eyes were dancing when I opened the basket and she saw all the wrapped packages just waiting for her.

Standing stiffly in front of me, Allie repeated her verse and Scripture reference. "Great, Allie. You can pick a present," I told her.

She was so excited as she selected one present from all the others. Her eyes sparkled as she tore the paper off. With her squeal of delight I knew I had found a good way to get the Word of God in her heart.

Nicole was just as eager. Her verse was simpler, since she was only five, but her excitement and enthusiasm matched Allie's. She danced as she unwrapped her present. As she stood in front of me examining her gift, I could see how proud she was for saying her Scripture and getting her present.

Now my grandchildren are coming with four or five verses memorized. It is a challenge to keep my basket filled. What better reward as I see those verses building a godly foundation in their lives. That old picnic basket has a brand new life.

Prayer Times

I was shocked and delighted by the question that my eighteen-year-old granddaughter had just asked: "Grandma, how can I pray for you?"

Erin and I had been talking on the phone for a long time about college life—its struggles and challenges. Many times at the close of our phone conversations over the years I had ended our time by saying, "Erin, I am praying for you." Now Erin was asking me to share my life struggles with her, and she was doing it using the question I had so often used with her.

As I held the receiver in my hand for those brief seconds, I felt compelled to think about what else I could do to impact the lives of Erin and my grandchildren for eternity. Maybe I should make a job description of an ideal grandparent and compare it to my life. It should help me be more effective in the coming years. The Lord was showing me he had put me in the lives of my grandchildren to help fulfill his purpose. "Yes, Erin, here's how you can pray for me. . . ."

Praying together with a grandchild develops a wonderful bond and trust. He will know he can always count on you. She will be honored by being asked to pray for you. It will have particular impact if you ask a grandchild to pray for you about an opportunity to witness to someone about Christ. Later you can share how that meeting went.

Travel Times

I have had the blessing of taking my older grandkids on trips to other countries. These weren't just sightseeing tours, but times to visit mission locations and see what the Lord is doing. We spend our time meeting the local people, seeing their needs and challenges, and sharing with each other how these encounters make us feel. Since God brought us here, obviously he wants us to do something about the conditions and opportunities.

We talk about what we see and decide what the Lord wants us to do. We do what we can there, then plan what we can do when we return home. These are times to talk about how God works—building blocks in their walk of faith and in our relationship.

Adding to the Legacies for Your Children

Many different individuals in the extended family can have input into your children's lives. Grandparents, aunts and uncles, cousins, and "step" relatives in your family network all have unique gifts to give. Some will see their role, and others will need your encouragement and direction. Working together with them, you can help shape the legacy they will leave to your children. Here are some ideas.

Mail

E-mail is great. It's easy to stay in touch by e-mail or even by snail mail. (I just heard the term "knee" mail. Praying for my grandkids now has a new name.) The beauty of mail is that because the message is written down, it can be saved and treasured.

Ask your godly relatives to write to your children about how God is directing them. How are they seeing people in their lives through the eyes of Jesus Christ and responding to what they see? Because you are training your children to see the people around them, you can ask your relatives to write about the ethnic people in their community and their connections with them. They'll need feedback as to how their letters are impacting your children. Let them know that through this simple act they are one of the Lord's tools in raising up those precious kids of yours.

Theme Trips

Do your children have a grandpa or grandma, aunt or uncle, who can take them fishing? It is really special for them to have a relative teach them to fish. Fishing is a marvelous opportunity to talk about the famous fishermen in the Bible. Jesus was very involved with fishermen and their boating adventures. When they return home, you can talk about when Jesus was asleep in the boat and the storm came up, frightening the disciples. You might even act this one out.

Try the story of Peter walking on the water. Act it out. When Peter saw Jesus what courage did it take to get out of the boat? Why did Peter start to sink? There is a lot to talk about here. Review those stories of Jesus and the fish dinners. Even the story of the boy with two fish and five small loaves of bread can be a learning experience. You might want to have bread and fish for lunch to see how far it will go.

How about a mountain climbing trip? Jesus went to the mountain to pray, and on one of those trips he fed five thousand people. You can tell the story of Abraham and Isaac on Mount Moriah or about Moses on Mount Sinai. Retelling these stories after an actual mountain climbing trip makes them more meaningful.

Family Stories

Grandparents, aunts and uncles, and other family members have stories to share from their childhood. Your children have probably never heard them. They don't know about their childhoods, mothers and dads, churches, or schools. These relatives can tell your children how they became a Christian and how old they were. How they learned about the Great Commission. Those growing-up stories are so totally different from anything your children experience today.

If family members have stories about not growing up in a Christian home, you can use these to talk about the extra blessing it is to have Christian parents.

Present-day stories of how God is leading are important as well. I often have special encounters (I call them divine appointments) that the Lord has put before me. As I tell these stories to my grandchildren, they can better understand how the Lord is with me all the time. I tell them how he prepares the way ahead for me. My stories of God's care add to the value they place on God in their lives. They can learn to look for divine appointments too.

Mom and Dad, pick up the phone. Call those grandparents, aunts, uncles, and cousins that are Christians. Tell them you want to talk about their influence. It's time to plan for generational blessings—part of the many stories in the Old Testament. Make it a part of your family. Make those legacies count for your children. They last forever.

THINGS YOU CAN DO AS A FAMILY

1. Discuss as a family how to involve grandparents, aunts and uncles, cousins, and any "step" relatives in your Great Commission family.
2. Talk to extended family members about what they have to share and how they would most like to share those things with your children.
3. Schedule and plan times for your children with these extended family members. Let the family members in on your desire to include them in your Great Commission emphasis.

147

4. Encourage grandparents to write out their most significant life stories, and arrange a special night when they bring these stories to be read aloud to your children.
5. Make a scrapbook for each child of the stories and expeditions with their extended family members.

THE ROLE
OF THE CHURCH

The church, a place of joy! A place of contagious excitement about being part of the family of God! Can you imagine that—a part of the family of God? What a privilege. What an honor. What a joy to gather in one room to worship him, the Creator, the Almighty.

But wait—there's more to it. In a family, everyone has responsibilities. Your church as part of God's family has responsibilities too. Here's the main one: This God who loves us and whom we love gave all of us, including our churches a suggestion—no, a command—to go, tell, and bring others into this family.

"Sure," I say to Jesus. "Why not? If it is good for us, it will be good for our church too. Yes sir, I believe that is what you want all of your family, your church people, to do. That sure looks like your number one command, so get me started on your assignment for our church. Send me in the right direction.

"As I look at what your disciples did after you left them, Jesus, it seems we must do the same thing. Let's see, Phillip headed south. He met this Ethiopian man and told him about you. Then he kept going, telling everyone he met about you. Peter headed over to Joppa and found some people just waiting to hear about you. That was just the beginning for him. He wasn't afraid to tell people he was your disciple, like he did the night you were captured by the soldiers. John got busy preaching in Jerusalem, and he ended up on the Isle of Patmos. He just wouldn't keep quiet about the Lord. Stephen, Barnabas, and Paul started sharing the message boldly. Being stoned took courage and faith. Lydia got involved, too, as did Silas and Mark and Priscilla and Aquila. Wow! That was some church. They got busy obeying. They knew that their number one priority was to 'go' and 'make' disciples of all nations" (see Acts 1:8).

Twenty centuries later, "go" and "make" disciples is still the number one priority. God's church is to do and be what the church was after Jesus returned to heaven. "Go" means around our town, our state, our country, and our world. Go to people of every race, every color, every language. Like an artist, we're creating a mosaic. God's church is a mosaic.

I shared this mosaic concept, that a church is a composite of many colors of people that together forms a whole, with Joe, an elder in a church. "Hmm," he said, "you don't understand. Our church is a carefully structured set of programs. There is the worship service and worship committee, Sunday school and the Christian education department, the stewardship team that takes care of the finances, the pastoral care team that helps meet needs, and the evangelism thrust. Of course, we have missions too. We push missions once a year and sometimes twice. Isn't that what a church is supposed to do?"

"Great, Joe!" I replied. "These programs are wonderful. The important clue to the value of all you said is whether all the people who are involved in these programs understand the purpose Jesus gave us for a church—to go and make disciples. Here's what I mean. The worship committee must bring this 'go' and 'make' into their program. They have a key role in helping the church focus on its purpose.

"Then, Joe," I continued, "the Christian education leaders can have lots of fun with this 'go' and 'make' too. It won't matter what the age of the class or group; Jesus' basic command is for everyone, always. It's what they really want to do anyway. It's their purpose, right? Classes can partner with missionaries. Leaders can plan parties for guests of other ethnic origins right there in town. Children's teachers can find books that offer ideas for mission fun. [One good resource is *Missions Made Fun for Kids* by Elizabeth Whitney Crisci.] Teachers and leaders all can bring this 'go' and 'make' into their lessons and action plans.

"There's more, Joe. The stewardship team should enjoy their part in the process too. 'Go' and 'make' can't happen as effectively without money. When the stewardship team gets excited about reaching the world, they will find ways to increase their church's giving from the 10 percent most churches start with up to 50 percent, in some cases. Here's an example. I know of one church that is building a much-needed addition to their facility. How are they doing it? They are telling the congregation that 50 percent of the funds raised for their new building is going to missions. People like that! It makes obeying the Great Commission exciting and challenging.

"Some churches have a 'faith promise' to enable all members of the congregation to test their faith in providing funds for missions. When members promise by faith that they will give a certain amount to missions this next year as the Lord gives it to them, they do spend some time on their knees. I think the Lord likes that.

"Pastoral care works two ways too, Joe. Yes, we need a pastor who weeps with us when we weep and rejoices with us when we rejoice. Also, at times we need to send our pastor to see the world that we are trying to reach. A congregation needs a leader whose purpose is to challenge his people to 'go' and 'make.' How rewarding it is to send a pastor to go see a part of the world through the eyes of Christ, to see 'the multitude and have compassion on them,' and then return to tell the congregation about it. Sending a pastor to care for those outside the church as well as those inside helps keep the church's number one priority number one.

"Evangelism? Yes. We want to reach people right around our home. We want to bring them to the Lord. We want to bring them into the family of God. Showing them love and care makes them ask why we would do this for them. Just yesterday a woman told me that the reason she and her husband came to my church and gave their hearts to the Lord was because someone invited them and sat with them in the service. That was easy evangelism!

"Outreach, Joe? Yes. That's part of our calling as a church too. Here's how one church responded in a big way to the question of a four-year-old boy. He and his mom were watching the news of the tragedy of families having to flee for their lives from war-torn Kosovo. Looking tearfully into his mother's eyes, he asked, 'Mommy, it's so sad. What can we do to help? Can we bring them here?' That mom went to the pastor who then went to the church with the little boy's question, and six months later a group from the church was at the airport welcoming a Muslim family of five to America. This church made outreach come alive in a new way through their response to Jesus' command, and they have changed the lives of those five war refugees."

Joe was amazed to hear all that I shared. He hadn't thought of his church's role in such sweeping perspectives. It was clear by the look on his face that he wanted to talk with his church leaders.

A church that puts priority on the Great Commission will use that term repeatedly. It will challenge families to be Great Commission families. It will challenge young people to put the Great Commission first in their lives. It will send its people on short-term mission trips. It will send forth its own full-time missionaries. Its people will see the world through the eyes of Christ and "go" and "make." These modern-day disciples will help turn the world upside down for Jesus Christ.

Here's an example. A church that I have known over the last twenty years is continually moving forward with their missions program. They realize that children need to catch the vision for missions and have found ways to make that happen. Each Sunday school class takes two mission projects a year. These projects may involve a specific need of one of their missionaries or a "kid friendly" project. Raising money to buy chickens for people in Brazil, goats for people in India, gasoline for missionary pilots, or eye ointment for people in Tanzania helps the kids catch the fever and joy of servanthood. Every Sunday time is given for missions. It is not an option. It is an essential part of their gathering. Each class adopts a missionary family and every third Sunday a representative sends an e-mail and reads the latest one received.

As for the junior high and high school students, they start with "home missions." They too have special class projects and provide funds to meet missions needs. Beginning in the seventh grade they go to a farm in Mississippi where they live in the community and work on the farm. Here they begin to understand the difference in cultures and what basic food and housing is to poor dirt farmers. Later they head for Seattle, the city that attracts the greatest number of homeless young people in America, so they do street evangelism and bring the message of care and hope.

Every December the church hosts Spirit Village, an event that draws in the whole family for that one day. This festival presents a special need for each of the various missions the church supports. The high school students run the booths, clean up, and take ownership of the various missions projects. A special game is played that day called Missionopoly. This is the church's own mission version of Monopoly. (To learn how it works, contact Doug Calhoun, missions pastor at Christ Church Oak Brook, 31st and York Road, Oak Brook, IL 60523, phone 630-654-1882.)

If your church isn't a Great Commission church, the kind described here, maybe you need to talk with its leaders. After all, everyone has responsibilities in the family of God.

The church, a place of joy! A place of contagious excitement about being part of the family of God. What a privilege. What an honor. What a joy.

WHAT YOU CAN DO TODAY AS A FAMILY

1. List the programs in your church and identify the person in charge of each one.
2. Get a copy of your church's missions budget. What percentage of the total church income is it? Find out what it would take for it to increase.
3. Memorize your church's purpose statement.
4. Pray for your pastors, leaders, and teachers that their vision of the world will be ever increasing. Consider what challenges the Lord has waiting.

GOD'S MESSENGERS

I t's just an ordinary day. I'm busy writing. My flowers are yelling for water. There are errands to run . . . an ordinary day. But there is contentment. Peace. Comfort. Joy. I've not done everything right, but the Lord has made it work anyway. My three sons have their eyes on Christ. They are Great Commission kids—just big kids in their forties.

Find a comfortable chair and sit awhile. Put your feet up, and don't worry about the yard or the unopened briefcase or the laundry. Slow down and think about where your kids are right now in relation to all you've heard about in this book. And relax. Maybe you won't go to Kenya, Austria, or China like those families you read about in chapter 14. Aside from their missions work, one of the best things both families discovered on their journey was how to reconnect as a family, to spend time together, to put family first before all other distractions and obligations, and focus on their life mission—to be obedient to the Lord.

Are you just starting this process of becoming a Great Commission family? Kids still young? Great. You have some incredible adventures ahead. I hope this book has helped you start laying plans—what you want to do as a family, where you want to go, and how you will get there. You only go down this path once, you know. Be adventuresome.

If your kids are tweens or teens, you are a very busy person. Stop! Schedule a family meeting. Talk and pray about what kind of family you *really* want to be in the next two or three years—or however many years you have before the kids are gone from your home. Serious discussions. But you only live this life once. You can't go back.

If your kids are grown and having their own families, be the thoughtful and benevolent grandparent with a legacy to pass on to those grandkids. Talk to your kids about those precious years they will have with their kids. You are not in charge, but you can encourage and support and pray.

While you are still in that comfortable chair, think for a minute about those twelve stammering, fearful men who followed Jesus when he walked on the earth. God sent his only Son to bring us salvation, and look who he used to help get the job done. Not anybody important. No one considered outrageously successful. Some common fishermen. A tax collector. Workers. Ordinary. Never had a course in public speaking. Just obedient. Yet they set the course for changing the world.

That was two thousand years ago, and God has used ordinary people through the years since then. There was a time for the disciples, and then for Paul and Barnabas, Saint Augustine, Jonathan Edwards, Martin Luther, John Calvin, George Fox, John Wesley, John Knox, D. L. Moody, Billy Sunday, Bill Bright, Francis Schaeffer, and Billy Graham.

They accomplished much in their times, but this is your time. Yours—to change the world. You can do it by investing in your kids. By being a Great Commission family. Your family, in spite of or because of your unique circumstances, can be a family of vision and determination and love and obedience to our Lord and Master. This is *your* day and *your children's* day to be God's disciples. Look up, reach out, and find your part in taking the Great Commission to those who are yet waiting to hear.

I challenge you to pull out a poster board. Write at the top "God's Messengers." Then list the disciples' names and other names of those you admire for their service to God. Now comes the important part. Add each of your family members' names. What do you think of that? Look good? Frame it. Gather your family together to pray over it, then hang it on the wall, somewhere prominent, where everyone can see it.

You and your family are the Lord's disciples, chosen by him to carry his message to the people of this world. Chosen by him—Almighty God.

NOTES

Chapter 1

1. Cornerstone Properties, Inc. Indianapolis, Indiana, used by permission.

2. *Merriam-Webster's Collegiate Dictionary*, tenth edition (Springfield, Mass.: Merriam-Webster, Inc.), s.v. "mission."

Chapter 2

1. David B. Barrett, Todd M. Johnson, and George T. Kunan, eds., *World Christian Encyclopedia* (Oxford: Oxford University Press, 2001) and David B. Barrett and Todd Johnson, *World Christian Trends* (Pasadena, Calif.: William Carey Library, 2001).

Chapter 12

1. Compassion International, 12290 Voyager Parkway, Colorado Springs, CO 80921, www.compassion.com, 800-336-7676; World Vision, P.O. Box 9716, Federal Way, WA 98063-9716, www.worldvision.org, 888-511-66598; India Gospel League, 6432 Hendrickson Road, Middletown, OH 46044, www.IGLworld.org, 513-422-1393.

Donna Thomas, founder of Christian Vision Ministries, has been ministering in the United States and in China, India, Russia, Egypt, Sri Lanka, Philippines, and across Latin America since the 1960s. Donna and her late husband, Chuck, parents of three sons, founded Project Partner with Christ, through which they led more than six thousand people to train pastors; construct churches, schools, and clinics; and partner with productive national leaders throughout the world. Donna is the author of *Climb Another Mountain* and a short-term missions journal, *Through the Eyes of Christ*. She speaks frequently to audiences worldwide and lives in Carmel, Indiana.

www.cvministries.org